Feel Good

Change The World™

A Career and Life Game Change

Make The Most Of Your Life By Changing
The way you live your life and manage your career

Jonathan Blain

Cover: © Jonathan Blain 2016
Cartoons: Roy Nixon
Illustrations: Presenter Media/ Flat Icon - Agreement ID I-7M80U-J4A03AM
Typesetting: Thea Tagulao and Irfan Idrees
Jonathan Blain Logo: Paul Barclay, Dartmouth, Devon, UK

JONATHAN BLAIN Moving The World

WHAT OTHERS ARE SAYING

"An uplifting book that offers a thought-provoking perspective on life and shows that you can do good while also doing good business."

John Timpson, CBE, Chairman of Timpson Group, Author and The Daily Telegraph Newspaper Columnist

"Jonathan is right when he says we need more wisdom, love and imagination. Making change happen needs conviction of the individual, as well as the enthusiasm and trust of the leaders. This book highlights how small steps can bring us forward, and how much energy good humour gives us. Spending most of my life in politics and the service of others, I am convinced this book will make you feel good and help you to positively change the world."

Erna Hennicot-Schoepges, Ex-President of Luxembourg Parliament, Mayor of Walferdange, Member of the Parliamentary Assembly of the Council of Europe, and of the European Parliament, Professor at the Conservatory of Luxembourg, Concert Pianist, Founder of University of Luxembourg, Mother, Wife and recipient of multiple awards and decorations internationally. Author of a number of books and articles on subjects ranging from politics, human rights, religion, and education.

"It is the imperative of our time to inspire each other to help make a difference and find positive solutions to the global challenges we now face. Jonathan's book describes many of these challenges. I particularly like his suggestion that each and every one of us should seek to make a difference which is not only good for us, but can help to positively change the world. I support the view that more wisdom, love and imagination would be a good thing."

Satish Kumar, A former monk and long-term peace and environment activist, author and editor of Resurgence magazine from 1973 - 2016.

WHAT OTHERS ARE SAYING

"Jonathan is an extreme Game Changer on The GC Index®. Our academic research on Game Changers, shows that they are the ones who have the propensity to change landscapes and move the human race forwards; but they cannot do it alone. Game Changers see possibilities where others do not, often driven by frustrations with the status quo. As with all Game Changers, Jonathan has generated the initial spark of creativity but it will take others who read this book to help make his ideas a reality."

Nathan Ott, CEO of The GC Index®.

"Jonathan has always been at the forefront of thought leadership and this body of work provides a rigorous, insightful and above all actionable guide as to how we can make a difference and change the world we live in"

Paul Bennett, Director of Executive Education at Southampton Business School & Previously at Henley Business School and a Keynote Speaker.

DEDICATION

I dedicate this book to people all over the world, who want to make the most of their life. People who dare to dream and believe that they could have a better career and a better life, and who have high hopes, real desires and aspirations that lie buried deep within them, that when realised will set them free, and enable them to fulfil their destiny, to be who they are really meant to be, to live their life with meaning and purpose. When this is achieved, they will get to live the life and career of their dreams, and have the perfect work / life balance, whilst simultaneously making a difference to others and the wider world.

I also dedicate this book to my family, particularly the women and girls who are closest to me, my mother Neva, my sister Deborah, my mother in law Betty, my wife Jenny, and our three beautiful daughters, Kezia, Xanthe and Talia. I love you all, you all inspire me!

CONTENTS

What Others Are Saying
Dedication
Author Introduction
Preface
Instructions for getting the most out of this book
Guiding Principles

| 1 | Introduction – An Issue of Life and Death Importance .... 19 |

Making the most of your life
Who this book was written for
Problem or challenge? Want to achieve more? Not sure?
What this book should do for you
The three core foundations of the Career and Life Game Change System

Change how you see things
Change what and how you think
Change what you do
The Blain Change Framework™
See the big picture and join the dots

| 2 | Living in an unprecedented time in human history .... 55 |

1. Exponential Rate of Progress and Change
2. Global Population Explosion
3. Exponential Growth in Knowledge
Today in context of evolution
Have lessons from older times been lost?
Are the young beginning to know more about the world than the old?

CONTENTS

The balance of opportunity versus threats in the modern world
 Economic Issues
 Political Issues
 Social Issues
 Environmental Issues
 Individual Issues
Take the way you live your life and manage your career to the highest level
 The best investment you can make is in yourself

3 The Author's Final Wake Up Call 107

Authors story
 Deciding to become the author of my own life story / life
 movie   Discovering what the world looks like from different
 perspectives

 How real life can sometimes be stranger than fiction
 Discovering myself
 Hitting rock bottom and discovering my true life purpose
 The search for deeper understanding leading to exploration and
 discovery
 Gaining a new perspective on life
 Belief in a need for a new enlightenment
 Wisdom, Love and Imagination

4 Your career and life journey 133

Your life and career
Be prepared for an onion
Take the red pill like in the film The Matrix
Consciousness and Questions
Thoughts on us as individuals, other people, the world and the universe

CONTENTS

Destiny Versus Free Will Conundrum
Universal forces that can enhance your life
Overcoming setbacks and challenges

5 Career and Life Game Change System – Introduction 173

Career and Life Game Change
The meaning and purpose of your life
In Control or Out of Control
Choose to be in control of your life and become a "leader in life"
Key goals that should be central to your life and should guide everything that you do
Start with why?
The Three Levels You Can Live Your Life At
    1.Functional / Tactical Level
    2.Transformational Level
    3.Transcendent Level
Human Beings not Human Doings

6 Take Control of Your Life and Career 209

Become The Author of Your Life Story, Script Writer and Director of Your Life Movie and CEO of Your Life
Your career and life mission control
    Sample Life and Career Planning Report:
The make a difference revolution

7 Your Identity – Making an Inner Journey 223

You have to know your true identity to know what you truly want

CONTENTS

8   **Making the Game Change**............................**235**

Change and break free from the herd
Take a holistic perspective and proactively manage your career and life

Be who you really are
Orientate your life and career around what is most important
Increase your consciousness
Embrace a new enlightenment
Choose to live your life at a higher level
Know why now is a unique time in human history
Recognise that humanity and the world are on the knife edge of crisis

Develop a deep curiosity and go on an inner journey
Put everything on the table that can help you and overcome the barriers and blockers
Work on your life and career not just in them
Discover your true authentic self and be who you truly are
Don't be like the majority have the courage to positively change the status quo
Join me and let's spread light into the world
Be aware of the dodgy parts of the self-help industry
Invest in yourself
10 Steps to Specifically Achieve the Career and Life of Your Dreams
> Step 1 - Make the choice to take control and become a leader in life
> Step 2 - Work out who you really are and document it
> Step 3 - Work out what you really want and document it
> Step 4 - Reality Check what you want with real world to come up with final goals

CONTENTS

Step 5 - Create a strategy of how you are going to achieve your goals

Step 6 -Translate your strategy into plans you can implement

Step 7 -Take action

Step 8 -Measure Results

Step 9 -Make improvements and changes as required

Step 10-Repeat the process on a regular basis

Afterword

Next Steps

About Jonathan Blain

Acknowledgements

Index

Final Thoughts

Notes

AUTHOR'S INTRODUCTION

"I'd like to invite you to join the Feel Good Change The World Movement.

You can feel better and change the world by helping yourself and helping others. Together we can make the world a sustainable and a better place.

You can make a massive difference, this book will show you how".

JONATHAN BLAIN™   *Moving The World*

f   Facebook.com/FeelGoodChangeTheWorld

y   @FeelGoodChange

in   Group: "Feel Good Change The World"

You Tube   Look Out For Us on You Tube

@   jonathan@FeelGoodChangeTheWorld.com

www   FeelGoodChangeTheWorld.com

AUTHOR'S INTRODUCTION

Why?

In everything that I do, I seek to be a force for good, to discover and use wisdom, love and imagination, and to help others to:

Achieve More, Be More, Do More, Have More, Know More, and Make a Bigger Difference.

Through my work, I intend to create an enabling, uplifting and positive revolution in the world, where people get to: see, think and act differently, so they can make things better for themselves, others, future generations and the entire world. Feel Good and Change the World!

Overview of My story

When I was young I used to like watching movies, and I decided I wanted to have the sort of exciting, adventurous and rewarding life that I saw people in the movies having. I quickly realised that this life wasn't going to be laid on for me, so I set about becoming the author of my own life story, and director of my own life movie. The result was that I gained a huge amount of experiences, both good and bad. I experienced some massive highs and lows, had plenty of real life adventures, made and lost millions, found myself in many life threatening situations, including being shipwrecked in mid-Atlantic, and at one time reached rock bottom. A massive curiosity, led me on a journey of discovery; I wanted to understand the meaning and purpose of life, and how we can all make the most of our lives and our time on earth. That journey led me to an epiphany that transformed my life. I had a strong feeling that everything I had ever done, experienced and achieved, was part of a lifetime apprenticeship, to prepare me to help others on their life journey. My ego gave way to humility, as I discovered my destiny to become a servant for humanity, helping others.

AUTHOR'S INTRODUCTION

"Feel good and change the world"

"I imagine a peaceful world in harmony: environmentally, politically, economically, socially and individually. I see us connected by the universal spirit of nature and humanity; a force for good, that is inspiring and positive. When passion, positive energy and enthusiasm flow, almost everything is possible and problems can be solved. I believe everyone deserves happiness and fulfilment. The greatest changes will come, not when world leaders rearrange things, but when each and every person, connects to their true life purpose, finds their life's work, and gives themselves to it, with all their heart, and seeks true wisdom. We should think, not what the world can do for us, but what we can do for the world and others, and in doing it, we can feel good, make a difference and positively change the world. Lots of small things added together can make a big difference. We are all equal as human beings, you matter as much as anyone else. Dare to dream, discover your destiny, make your biggest, best and highest contribution to the world, use your imagination, and remember you are not alone. Where there is a will, there is nearly always a way. Whenever there is darkness, light will always follow, never give up, unless there is no way forward, if that happens, reassess and come up with new goals that inspire you. Always make the most of every situation you find yourself in. Make every day count."

Jonathan Blain

PREFACE

In this book, you will discover that we are living in an extraordinary time in the history of humanity, for 3 primary reasons: 1. A massive explosion in global population, 2. An exponential rate of change and progress, and 3. A massive acceleration in the speed at which knowledge is doubling in the world. The consequence is that world is on a knife edge between great opportunity and also great threats, with the world being on the edge: 1. Economically, 2. Politically, 3. Socially, 4. Environmentally and finally 5. Individually. I believe all these things are connected.

At an individual level, most people are experiencing a plethora of issues and challenges, that at the deepest level, goes to the core of who we really are, what we really want, even why we are alive. There is an epidemic of pressure, stress, anxiety and issues regarding our general mental health and physical condition and overall wellbeing.

Against this backdrop, I believe now is a time when we need new thinking, new ideas and new solutions, driven by a new enlightenment, which is based on three tenets: 1. Wisdom, 2. Love and 3. Imagination.

In essence, we need a to game change our approach to the way we live our lives, and manage our careers, so that we can make the most of our lives, and our time on earth. To do this, we need to change three fundamental things: 1. The way we see things, 2. What and how we think? and 3. What we do. To enable these changes, we need to increase our consciousness, to develop a deeper curiosity, and an ability to challenge our own knowledge, beliefs and assumptions. We have to be open minded, and ultimately prepared to break free from the herd mentality, that forces us to subconsciously do similar things to the majority, without even realising that we are doing it.

The modern world is orientated around the subconscious pursuit of success, which at its core is represented by money and wealth, which enables you to buy stuff and to have choices.

PREFACE

Whilst money is needed, there is no doubt about that, it is not the end goal. The end goal should be 1. Happiness, 2. Fulfilment and 3. Making a difference, which are the primary things you need to focus on. The biggest mistake is to believe that money makes you happy on its own, it doesn't; many super wealthy people have been so unhappy, they have taken their own lives.

Altruism and making a difference, is not only good for the beneficiaries, it also good for you. I believe it is also our obligation and responsibility to future generations, and something that will also give you peace of mind, and help you to sleep well at night. We should together look to hand over the world to the next generations in as good, or ideally, a better condition than we inherited it. Doing your part towards this, will help you to be truly happy, and to be successful beyond your hearts desire as well. "Give and you will receive"; what you give freely to others and the wider world, with a good heart, and with expectation of nothing in return, has a habit of bringing good things back to you with interest. This is a philosophy that you can adopt as a new way of life, that will make your life better.

You need to think holistically, and see the bigger picture, as well as putting your whole life under the microscope.

To make the most of your life, you need to know what you really want, so that you can discover the best way of getting it. The problem is, that all too often, we don't really know what we want, and often what we think we want, isn't what we actually want. To know what it is that you truly want at the deepest level, you need increased consciousness, self-understanding and awareness, and to get to the core of your true identity. The best way of doing this is to go on an inner journey of introspection and discovery, to gain a deep understanding about all aspects of your identity. This will enable you to work out what is important and not important for you, so that your goals can be crystal clear, and that you can apply your efforts in the right direction. To do this,

PREFACE

means taking the way you live your life, and manage your career to the highest level. In doing this, you can do more, have more, know more, be more and make more of a difference. You can not only change your life, you can positively transform it, and even transcend to the highest level of human existence if you set your mind to it. In effect, you have to play two games; an inner game, and an outer game in the real world.

It is an exciting journey, full of possibility, I hope you are up for the challenge. The truth is that most people won't be, they will follow the majority, doing broadly the same things. They will resist change, they will close their hearts and minds to new possibilities, and won't be prepared to do what it takes to live their life at a higher level; what is worse, they are unlikely to see this is what they are doing. Only you can decide what is right for you, but if you decide to live your life at a higher level, you can join the small community of like-minded people, who not only aspire to make the most of their lives, but who actually try to turn their dreams into reality, and to make their highest and best contribution to the world.

Feeling good more of the time, in fact not just feeling good, but feeling great, even awesome, is the prize. The way that you can achieve this, is to take the way you live your life and manage your career to the highest level, and also be a force for good in the world, to make a difference, and in doing so, you'll create a positive ripple, that can contribute to positively changing the entire world. The truth is, that small things that you can easily do, matter much more than you think they do, and you are also way more powerful and capable than you think you are.

You will need to see and discover the truth, make the connections and change the game.

GETTING THE MOST OUT OF THIS BOOK

To get the most out of this book, you need to understand that the overarching aim of this book is to help you to positively transform your life and your career, in other words, to create a profound, positive and transformational change, that will enable you to eliminate many of the things that are wrong in your life, gain things of your wildest dreams, and make other things better. You'll discover that in achieving these things, you can be a force for good, and make the world a better place too. When you get it right, what is good for you, is good for others and the wider world.

To achieve these things, you need to read this book in order, and put into practice what you have learnt. It is important you read it in a linear way, because the book is following a logical process, where you need to understand one concept, before moving onto the next. Once you have read it for the first time, you can then refer to different sections on their own.

This book is intended to connect with your heart and soul, to trigger ah ha moments that resonate with your logic as well as your inner self, and result in career and life transforming changes.

It is about helping you to discover the truth about the most important things in life, and helping you to lift the fog of deception and illusion, that is capable of tricking us all. The hope is that you will be able to see clearly, what is truly important to you and what is not, what should be a priority and what shouldn't, and finally, how you can make the changes you need, to get what your heart truly desires.

GETTING THE MOST OUT OF THIS BOOK

I also hope that you'll achieve an epiphany, "a moment of sudden and great revelation or realisation", that will change everything for you. Sadly, not everyone will, you've got to be ready to receive it. If you don't achieve it on your first read, please don't be disillusioned, try reading it again, and if that still doesn't work, go back to your life, reflect on it, and come back to the book in sixth months or a year or more. You'll discover later in the book, that I didn't get it to begin with, not the first time, or even the second time. It took me a long time to truly wake up the reality. I've come to the conclusion that I am not alone in having that experience.

In the book, you will discover a section on consciousness; the intention is that the first part of the book will help to increase your consciousness about careers, life, the state of the world, and the extraordinary opportunities and challenges facing humanity as a whole. This increased consciousness will give context and insight to your own life journey, that will enable you to make a shift and game change, and positively transform your own life and career.

You have to:
1. See the truth.
2. Make the connections.
3. Change the game.

"You are not a drop in the ocean, you are an entire ocean in a drop"
Jalaluddin Rumi

GUIDING PRINCIPLES

I want to help you discover how good you really are, what you are capable of, what is possible for you, and teach you how to change your game, so that you can aim higher, achieve more, be happier and more fulfilled, and make a real difference in the world. I believe you deserve to feel alive, to feel energised, and to align your life and your career to your passions, so that you can achieve the quality of life and lifestyle that you desire.

This book sets out to transform your life, and the lives of millions of other people, by enabling you to take control, live your life at a higher level, so that you can achieve a great life, a great career, and a perfect work / life balance.

This book is driven by a set of guiding principles:

1. *To make as big a difference to you as possible.*
2. *To be 100% grounded in reality and the real world as I perceive it.*
3. *To be 100% honest.*
4. *To be driven from a perspective of deep genuine caring and a position of service.*
5. *To offer a new, different and better perspective.*
6. *To be at the leading edge / vanguard of positively influencing the quality of lives and careers.*

"You are much more important, significant, powerful and capable than you think you are."

CHAPTER 1

AN
ISSUE
OF LIFE
AND DEATH
IMPORTANCE

"We are all born and we will all die, in between is our life, we have a choice to waste it or make the most of it; I think our life is a precious gift, and that we are all meant to make the most of it."

When it comes to importance, there is nothing more important than matters of life and death. If you witnessed a major car accident, where you can see that people are seriously injured, you are not going to delay calling for an ambulance. You are not going to go swimming in the sea when you can see a load of hungry looking Great White Sharks circling just opposite the beach. You are not going to set out on a walk to the top of an exposed hill in the middle of a thunderstorm, where forked lightening is hitting the hilltop. You are not going to leave dangerous wiring in your house, or a faulty gas boiler unattended to. When it comes to avoiding imminent death, we will give it a high priority, because there is nothing more important than our lives, right?

Making the most of your life

MAYDAY... MAYDAY!

You instinctively know what is important and not important, don't you?

When it comes to living your life however, there is more to it than just existing like battery chickens living in a tiny cage, waiting for an inevitable death. Just existing and being alive on its own, for most people is simply not enough. A human life that involves just existing, can make you seriously unhappy, stressed and depressed; in fact, just existing has become such a problem for so many people, that many are choosing to commit suicide, rather than carrying on living. For some, death is better than life and that is a great cause for concern.

The problem was graphically illustrated at the Foxconn Factory in Shenzhen in China, where IPhones were made, where in one year, 14 people committed suicide, by jumping out of windows. At one time, 150 people staged a protest on the roof, threatening to commit suicide en mass, complaining about working conditions.

According to the UN Refugee Agency, more than 2,500 migrants and refugees died trying to cross the Mediterranean in rubber dinghies and rusting fishing boats, trying to reach Europe, in the first part of 2016. These people chose to knowingly risk their lives, rather than stay where they were. These situations might seem extreme, but now the biggest killer of men in the modern western world aged between 20 and 50 is thought to be suicide, and the biggest cause of death of adolescent girls used to be childbirth, but is now suicide. There is an epidemic of mental health, that is likely to affect pretty much all of us at some stage in our lives, caused by the pressures and challenges faced by many of us in the modern world.

The point I am making, is that the quality of all of our lives matters a great deal. Whilst you and your situation might be very different to other people, at the end of the day, we are all human beings sharing the experience of human life. I recently watched a BBC TV report where Prince Harry was talking about how mental wellbeing issues affects everyone, whether you are a prince or a pauper, whether you are rich or famous, or just an ordinary person, we are all just human beings; we arrive in the world with nothing, and leave with nothing. You don't need to look far, to see a host of rich and famous people whose quality of life, is not as good as it may seem from the outside, and many have either accidentally or deliberately taken their own lives like: actor Robin Williams, singers, Amy Winehouse, Michael Jackson, Prince and Witney Houston. Sarah Johnson was just 36, a wealthy and successful lawyer, who lived with her banker husband in a £12.5m house. She had three wonderful children who she loved very much, the youngest of which was just three, but an inquest heard that despite this, she felt her self-respect, self-esteem and dignity had all gone, so she jumped under a train to commit suicide.

The Clock is ticking - make the most of your lifetime!

I believe that your life is of supreme importance, as is everyone else's life. This book is about how we in the modern westernised world, can make the most of our time on earth; the certainty that we all have, is that are lives are finite, none of us can live forever. None of us know exactly how long we have got, but I believe we rarely think of our life as a whole, and we rarely do a good job of proactively and reactively managing our whole lives. I think our lives would be better if we did.

We don't arrive in this world with a handbook and a set of instructions. In our childhood, many decisions about the life we live, are not made by us, they are made for us. We are launched into adulthood onto certain career and life paths. I believe that many of these paths are not as good as they could be, and that by not making a choice to manage our whole life, we end up living lesser lives. Given how important our whole lives are, you would think we would give them much more attention than we typically do, but we get so caught up in day to day issues, and we are so influenced by the status quo, our upbringing, society and peers, that we don't recognise the opportunity we have to make the most of them.

It is quite remarkable how few people give any consideration at all, to trying to make the most of their whole life, by taking control of it and managing it. Somehow, day to day struggles and challenges, keep us busy, so busy in fact, that we can find it very easy to drift through life, wasting precious time, and not making the most of it. Often it takes something bad happening to act as a wake-up call. It could be a serious accident or illness, the loss of a loved one or someone you know, or even terrible global events, like natural disasters or terrorist attacks, that make you realise how precious your own life is. If someone is diagnosed with a terminal illness, it typically makes them really think about what is important to them. For young children in this situation, we feel a warm glow when we get to hear that their dreams have come true, whether it is a trip to Disneyworld, or a visit from their favourite celebrity. There is something particular heart-warming about charities like Make a Wish Foundation (www.make-a-wish.org.uk) whose aim is to grant magical wishes to enrich the lives of children and young people fighting life-threatening conditions.

If you are having a heart attack, saving your life is the most urgent priority, without doubt. If you were diagnosed with cancer and told you only had a few weeks or perhaps months to live, everything would change, you would have such clarity, about what was important, and what you wanted to do in the time you had left. At what point does making the most of your life become not so important; if you only had one year, two years, five years, ten years etc.?

We are typically so scared of death, we can't think about our own, therefore we put the prospect out of our mind, and waste so much of our life, doing things that are not important, and giving priority to the wrong things. What about your dreams, the really big ones that lie inside you, don't they deserve to see the light of day? Have you even got to the stage where you've stopped

> *We are typically so scared of our own deaths, that we don't realise how limited our time on earth is, and how precious each day is.*

dreaming? The late, formula one motor racing driver and world champion, James Hunt said: "the closer you are to death, the more alive you feel". It is a travesty if you wait until you are close to death to make the most of your life, firstly because there is no time left to do things, and secondly the older we get, the less our ability to do things that require physical peak. The film The Bucket List, starred Jack Nicholson and Morgan Freeman, who portrayed two terminally ill men, who went on a road trip with a wish list of things to do before they "kicked the bucket". You need, not just a bucket list of things to do in your lifetime, but a deep dive into what would make your life the best it could be in all respects, it is not just what you do, it is how you feel, who you are with, the contribution that you make and a whole lot more. Everyone is different.

It is not that we don't manage our lives at all, of course we do that, it is just we just don't do it as well as we could. Because most other people aren't actively managing their whole lives, we don't feel like we are missing out on anything, if everyone else was doing it, the likelihood is that we would too. There is a great opportunity for you to better manage your life.

Very few people ever think to themselves "how can I learn how to make the most of my life?" Some people will turn to a life coach, usually to help them solve a specific problem or issue. This book sets out to be very different from traditional life coaching, it aims to create a revolution, and help you to fundamentally "game change" your approach to living your life and the way that you manage your career. The book outlines a view of the world, that gives context to a "New Enlightenment™" and framework, that you can use to improve the quality of your life, and to help you to make the most of your time on earth.

A game change isn't a little change, it is a big fundamental change, with the intention of positively changing everything.

If you are a business owner, you might be familiar with advice that is often given by other successful business leaders, who say: "take some time to work on your business not just in it". What they mean by this, is that someone running a business, particularly a smaller business, is often so busy running the day to day operations, that they don't take the time to step back and work on the whole business strategically. This might mean thinking about the purpose of the business, the goals and objectives, planning a better, brighter future, perhaps working on your brand, creating vision, strategy and plans to make the business better. When you are trying to keep your business running, dealing with day to day problems, serving customers, managing staff or suppliers, you become so busy that you can't see what is going on. Sometimes in these situations business leaders miss important things, like collecting debts, seeing the business isn't profitable, and at worst, it can result in the business failing completely.

In effect, we have exactly the same issues with our life, we are so busy working in it, living it, consumed by day to day issues, challenges and pressures, that we don't take the time to step back, to work out what is going well and what isn't, what we really want, what problems we really have, and what strategies and plans can be adopted to make things better.

You are only likely to positively transform your life when you do this. Surely your life is important enough for you to make the time isn't it?

Who this book was written for

This book is for people who have the motivation to make the most of their life, and who are prepared to make changes to the way they live it and manage their careers, so that they can achieve the very best outcomes.
This book is written for 6 types of people:

MOTIVATION CAN COME IN ALL SORTS OF WAYS...

Your motivation to positively transform your life needs to come from within.

1. *Entrepreneurs, Business Owners and The Self Employed*
2. *Managers and Executives*
3. *Mothers and Fathers*
4. *College and University Students*
5. *Retired People*
6. *Anyone who is open minded*

Entrepreneurs, Business Owners and The Self Employed

Who have already taken charge of their own destiny, and who want to maximise their business success, whilst also achieving a great life.

Executives and Managers

Men and women who want to maximise their own career success, happiness and fulfilment, and possibly support others to achieve the same.

College and University Students

Typically, younger people who are starting out, who have got their entire lives and careers in front of them, who want to achieve the best life and career possible.

Mothers and Fathers

Whose lives change on becoming parents, who want to achieve not just great lives and careers for themselves, but who also want to do the best things for their family, and set their children on the best career and life paths.

Retired People

Whose main careers might have ended, but who still have a zest for life, and who are determined to make the next chapter of their lives one of the best.

Anyone

Anyone at all, of any gender, of any age, in any situation, and of any background who:

- *Wants to find the best solutions to problems, issues or challenges they may have in their careers and lives, or;*

- *Whose life and career is already great, who want to take them to the next level, to live life to the full, to make the most of their life, to be everything that they want to be, to live life on their terms, to achieve more, be more, experience more, have more, and maximise their happiness, fulfilment, career success and contribution or;*

- *Feels that something is not quite right with their life and career, and wants to discover what it is, if any-*

thing, and what they can and should do about it, to achieve the very best career and life possible.

Whilst everyone likes to think of themselves as being open-minded, being blunt, most are not. Being open minded, means being receptive to new ideas, that can result in a positive change to the status quo. People who have both accumulated life experiences, accepted leadership responsibilities and also been around long enough to experience challenges, that make them desire better ways, are at an advantage. If you don't have many experiences, you don't have the same frame of reference to draw upon.

If you don't have challenges or things you need to accomplish, you won't have the need for change, or as much motivation to discover better ways, and make the changes needed to get what you want.

You need to be prepared to be different, but the desire to conform will make that difficult

Whilst you might think that everyone would be receptive to anything that is new, different or better, they are often not, as many marketers have found to their cost. We human beings, struggle with change, particularly if it challenges or maybe conflicts with our view of the world, and our beliefs about how things should be. We are often, and perhaps rightly, highly sceptical of anything new, different, or purporting to be better. Our default position is usually to broadly do what the majority do; the truth is that most people are magnetically attracted to the status quo.

The subject matter of this book is pioneering, it is at the leading edge of progress, it sets out specifically to challenge the status quo, and make your life and your career better, regardless of where they are right now e.g. you might be reading this book with all sorts of problems issues or challenges in your career or life, or you might be in a situation where both your life and career are great, and you are just interested in making them even better.

Please don't be put off if you are young and experienced, as long as you are truly open minded, this book is for you, every much as it is for anyone else.

You are going to be presented with new ideas, new thinking and new solutions, but you won't achieve anything this book promises, if you don't put them into practice; change doesn't happen if you don't make it happen.

Problem or challenge? Want to achieve more? Not sure?

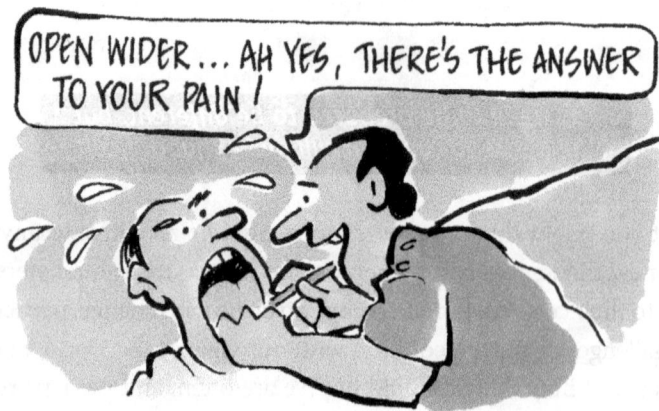

Something brought you to this page of this book, or to listen to these words if you are listening to an audio programme, at this point in time, and I'd like to hazard a guess that it was one of four primary reasons:

1. *You've got a specific problem, issue or challenge in your life or career right now, that you want and need to solve?*

2. *Your life and career is great, but you are interested in taking one or both of them, to an even higher level, to make them even better?*

3. *You have a niggling feeling that something is wrong with your life or career, but you are not quite sure what, or even if it is anything at all?*

4. *You've got an insatiable curiosity to explore new ideas, new thinking and new solutions, with a view to exploring whether they may be beneficial to you?*

It could well be, that more than one of these apply to you.

At first, it might seem that these four things are not related. What can someone who has real, perhaps even very serious, career or life, problems, issues or challenges, have in common with someone whose life and career is the complete opposite, and whose only desire is to make them even greater, and what have either of these types of people got in common with people who aren't sure they have a problem or issue at all, or people who just have a curiosity to see what new ideas are out there, that might help them?

The truth is that whatever your situation, the underlying desire is for improvement and discovering better ways, indeed the very best way to achieve whatever you want to achieve. If you take any life or career scenario, and apply it to different people, it can be perceived in very different ways, what is perceived as good for one person, can be perceived as bad by another, it all comes down to expectations, beliefs, feelings, and perceptions. It is for this reason, that this book is written for all people regardless of their personal situation.

Whether the sun is shining in your career and life and you just want more, or if you have a problem to solve; the solution is the same

Whether you have a problem to solve, or simply want to make things better, this book offers a radical new approach. It is based on a view of life, careers and the world, and a philosophy and framework that be applied to multiple situations.

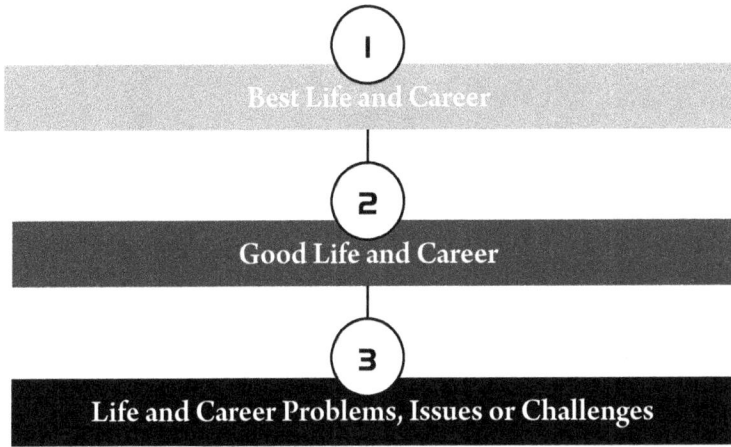

1 Best Life and Career

2 Good Life and Career

3 Life and Career Problems, Issues or Challenges

Imagine a line graph with failure at the bottom left, and success at the top right, or perhaps a scale of bad at the bottom left and good at the top right. What I hope you can understand, is that different people will have different perceptions about where they are on that graph. A billionaire who has lost most of his or her money, and is down to their last few tens of millions, might think their situation is really bad, but to someone with nothing, having tens of millions would be beyond their wildest dreams. I don't suggest what is good or bad for you, only you can define that. I assume your position could be anywhere on that imaginary graph, this book is intended to help you to move yourself to a higher and better position, regardless of your starting point.

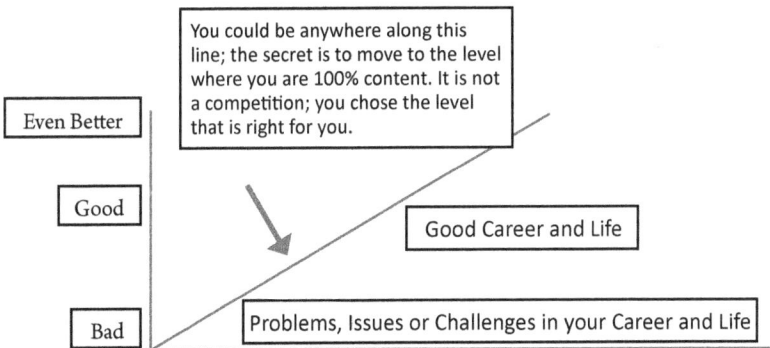

You could be anywhere along this line; the secret is to move to the level where you are 100% content. It is not a competition; you chose the level that is right for you.

Even Better

Good

Bad

Good Career and Life

Problems, Issues or Challenges in your Career and Life

We like to go Up not Down

Solving Problems and Making Things Better
1. Solution is the same
2. Only magnitude / distance is different

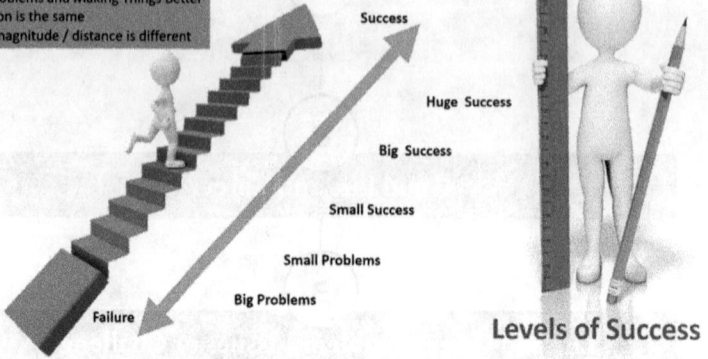

Success

Huge Success

Big Success

Small Success

Small Problems

Big Problems

Failure

Levels of Success

You have to define what success is to you

What this book should do for you?

This book offers you a new, different and better way of living your life and managing your career, so that you can make the most of your time on earth, and in particular be:

> 1. *Happier.*
> 2. *More fulfilled.*
> 3. *Make a bigger difference.*
> 4. *Achieve the career success you want.*
> 5. *Meet all your financial needs and desires.*

You'll discover a new surprising way of seeing things, that is likely to take what you know, believe and expect, and reframe it; it is like gaining awareness of the problem behind the problem, or the issue behind the issue.

I hope this book will be a catalyst to positively transform your own life, but also that it will be a catalyst for a new movement of like-minded people, that will bring positive changes to not just their own lives, but also other people's lives, and in time the wider world. This book is about positively changing the status quo, in terms of how we in the modern western world, typically approach living our lives and managing our careers.

Your life and your career are intertwined, there is an interdependence

Is your career not everything you want it to be?

between them. Some people will see their careers as simply a means of earning money, so that they can then live the life that they want, but our careers generally, account for a significant part of our lives, and are typically much more than simply being a financial powerhouse; they become integral to our identity, our quality of life, and our lifestyle, and therefore it makes sense to consider them together.

It is travesty to not make the most of your life, to live it to the full, to be all that you can be, to do what you want to do, to experience all that you want to experience and to make you best and highest contribution.

The three core foundations of the Career and Life Game Change System

The secondary subtitle of this book is: "make the most of your life, by changing the way you live your life and manage your career". "Change" is the key word, and change means "an act or process through which something becomes different".

There are three core elements of change, that are the foundation of this book and the "Career and Life Game Change System".

1. *Change how you see things*
2. *Change what and how you think*
3. *Change what you do.*

Sometimes you read things or hear things, and it washes over you, you don't realise the importance and significance; the message goes metaphorically in one ear, and out the other! These three things are so important, you mustn't let that happen. When the penny drops for you, there will be no going back. When early sailors eventually realised the world wasn't flat, and that they weren't going to sail off the edge, they could never go back to their old beliefs and fears.

You might be familiar with the farm of diamonds story? It is supposed to be true, but I am not sure if it is, but the essence of the story was that a farmer living in Africa heard about people finding diamonds and gaining great wealth. He was earning a measly living from his farm, so he sold up to go diamond hunting. He never found any, and disillusioned and broke he threw himself into a river and drowned, meanwhile the person who had brought his farm discovered that the farm was covered in diamonds. It turned out to become one of the richest diamond mines the world has ever known.

My advice to you, is don't walk past these diamonds right here on these pages, please believe me when I tell you, that if you use these three simple things, you can change your life forever. They are your passport to a better life, if you use them wisely and remain persistent. If you are not prepared to consider doing this, there is little point reading the rest of this book, they are that significant. This is where your open-mindedness is tested.

Perhaps the best way of explaining this, is to tell you a short story. I once made £20 million in just nine months. At the start, I was in a fair bit of debt, and I wasn't earning very much, I was actually working out of my garage. It seems so improbable, that you think to achieve such a thing might be impossible, but the truth is I actually did it, and the way in which I did it was by simply:

> 1. *Seeing differently.*
> 2. *Thinking differently.*
> 3. *Acting differently.*

I think very few people, have made so much money, in such a short period of time. This story is not about making money, it about game changing.

I once studied psychology, and not even to a great depth, but it was one of the most profound life changing things that I have ever done. I discovered that two people could look at the same thing, and see something completely different; for me, that fact was a revelation. Seeing doesn't just have to be seeing with your eyes, it also represents a metaphor for perceiving. Just look at how two politicians can hold such diametrically opposed views on the same issue, with each being convinced they are right. One man's terrorist can be another man's freedom fighter. I think the late Nelson Mandela was a great example of this. He was a Nobel Peace Prize winner, and President of the Republic of South Africa, yet it was not until 2008, that he was taken off the USA Terror Watch List by George W Bush.

I am intrigued by optical illusions, particularly an example where an image of a dress went viral in 2015; some people would see the dress as white and gold, and others as a deep blue and black. You wouldn't have thought that such a thing could be possible, the colours are so vastly different.

Is the glass half full or half empty?

Sometimes it is difficult to differentiate between what is seeing and what it thinking, it is therefore difficult to look at them in isolation, they go hand in hand. A great example of seeing and thinking differently, is whether you see a glass as half full, or half empty. It is possible to see value in things where other people see little or no value, and it is also possible to see opportunity, where others see none. A man in Gaza sold a Banksy painting for approximately $175 when Banksy paintings have been known to sell for hundreds of thousands of dollars, afterwards, he was naturally upset.

I am sure you are interested to know how I managed to make £20 million in nine months. I don't offer the story to you as a get rich quick scheme, that you can replicate exactly, but you can learn from the principles. Having money might give you choices, but on its own it doesn't bring joy and happiness, in fact it can sometimes bring the absolute opposite.

The starting point of this achievement is that I am a pioneer, visionary and game changer, so I have some advantage in having a natural ability to see, think and act differently, but it is something that you too can do, and this book is all about helping you to do it and understanding what is possible.

I learnt early on, that you can get what you want in life, if you are prepared to help other people get what they want; it is the essence of trade and value exchange. I also observed the way the world works, in particular how technology companies could grow quickly, make a lot of money, and be highly valued. Technology companies that achieved this, made money for the founders and external shareholders, they created jobs and opportunities for employees, and had a ripple effect, of not just adding value to customers, but also into filtering benefits into a wider economic eco-system. I also observed that there is an eco-system to support new technology companies to grow, that comprises of bankers, investors, analysts, accountants, solicitors, corporate advisers, financial markets, specialist PR and marketing companies etc. There is an interdependence between these organisations.

You have to see the game and understand how it works.

I'd written 8 books on the computer software SAP, and I was able to see how small and start-up companies had been able to grow quickly and profitably, and achieve incredibly high valuations. It is therefore not improbable that other new and early stage businesses in good market segments, with good propositions and people, could do the same. I had a business delivering SAP software related services, but I have always been good at seeing the big picture, and I could see that I was really into that market too late. I always feel that new things often arrive like a wave, that builds up getting bigger and bigger, but eventually the energy dissipates from it, and it dies down. Most people have little awareness and understanding of these waves. These waves are like a window of opportunity.

It was with some regret, that I felt I was very close to a huge fantastic wave, but I'd missed it, a bit like a surfer who fails to catch and ride the giant wave that comes along almost once in a lifetime. What I had done however, was to recognise the game. I knew that I too could play the game, but I needed another wave. I did my homework and it was obvious. The SAP software that I had written about, was part of a generic group of software referred to as ERP (Enterprise Resource Planning), which was also referred to as the "Back Office". I could see that the financial and technology analysts were also looking for the next big thing, and they had identified a new type of software referred to as CRM (Customer Relationship Management), which was also referred to as the "Front Office". The analysts were predicting that the CRM market was likely to be even bigger than the ERP market which was huge. They also identified the "mid-market" segment of that market, as the one likely to be the biggest. I happened to be a reseller of a mid-market CRM product called GoldMine. I contacted my publishers and got a contract to write another book on GoldMine Software, one of the "Complete Idiots Guides Series". I understand business and entrepreneurship, and I knew that there were a number of elements that I needed to complete, to create an investible proposition, that I could float on a stock market. I knew that I needed: ambition, vision and a believable story, a strategy of how to achieve the vision, credible plans that could show how the strategy could be implemented, strong leadership, a team, and advisers. I knew the plan was only as good as the weakest link, so I made sure that there were no weak links.

In just nine months start to finish, I achieved all the steps needed, and was successful in achieving the biggest ever IPO on the market, achieved in the shortest ever time frame, raising £5.4million for just 20% of the company, which made my shares worth £20m+. For every penny my share price moved, I made or lost circa £250K. Sadly the anticipated market failed to live up to expectations, and ultimately the business wasn't sustainable, but all businesses ventures carry risks, nevertheless achieving a record breaking IPO is no mean feat.

Times are different today, but start-up companies like Uber and Snapchat have reached Unicorn Status, which means valuations of over $1bn in very short time frames.

This book is not about entrepreneurship, although perhaps you are an entrepreneur yourself, and that is your career path. I've told you this story, not to recommend that you become and entrepreneur, or that you seek to be super wealthy, although you can if you wish, but I've told you, so that you can see what is possible when you see, think and act differently. This is just one of many examples of how I have used the concept of seeing, thinking and acting differently, to achieve extraordinary things in many other ways. You would be amazed at what is possible for you, if you can only embrace this simple concept. Here are some other examples:

- I once needed a job, but instead, I managed to persuade a FTSE 100 company to go into a joint venture business with me. They agreed to invest £500K, and installed me as Managing Director of a new business that I part owned, on a nice salary. I don't think many other people have done that!

- I once had a house that I couldn't sell, and felt I needed some publicity, so I managed to get more free publicity for the sale of my house than anyone has ever got before, including 2/3 of a page of editorial in the Sunday Times and the Saturday Telegraph, half a page on the Mail on Sunday, a 6-page feature article in a property magazine. Reuters did a TV story that was broadcast all over the world and lots more.

- I had never written a book before, yet I managed to write a book that became an international best seller, and was published by one of the world's biggest publishers, and was even endorsed by one of the Co-Founders of software giant SAP, who were then the world's third largest software company. I have since had my work endorsed by many top leaders.

- It is not just that I've used these concepts, countless other people have also. As well as writing books myself, I help other people to write books and also publish them. One of my first customers was Gary Dutton. He left school at 16 with no qualifications, his teachers told him he would amount to nothing, yet now he is worth approx. £130 million, by seeing, thinking and acting differently.

- Many years ago I met an 18 year-old girl who was sailing on her own around the UK. We became friends, and I helped her when she was largely unknown; ten years later, the BBC paid for me to go to Falmouth, and I was interviewed on her yacht, she had just become the fastest person to sail around the world, and was made the UK's youngest Dame.

- I once met a lady who said she was sad at the negative celebrity based television that was aired, she questioned why ordinary people weren't on TV and real life stories and issues discussed. I said don't complain, do something about it, she said, would you help me, and within 3 months we'd created a TV series called "The Life Show" involving ordinary people covering real life issues and stories. Over 100 people were involved, we had a professional production crew of up to 30, by partnering with an ex Sky News Cameraman, and it was all done on a shoestring.

I am not unique is seeing, thinking and acting differently, countless other people have learnt and done the same thing, to create extraordinary outcomes. Olympic Sprint Champion Michael Johnson, who won four Olympic gold medals, and eight World Championships gold medals. said: "People think what the majority do is right, but that is not necessarily the case. My technique was more efficient, but nobody had seen it before".

The truth is, you too can see, think, and act differently, and also achieve extraordinary things, in fact you don't even need to set out to achieve extraordinary things if you don't want to; it can enable you to achieve all sorts of things that you might not think are possible for you.

It seems like three simple things, seeing, thinking and acting different is easy and straight forward, but it often isn't. Subconsciously we all have an in built desire to want to fit it, to not stand out too much, to doubt ourselves so much, that we would rather conform, and be just like others, see things like others, think like others and act like others. Our education system and upbringing, and the society we live in, means that in the modern western world, we are highly unlikely to walk around town in loin cloths or bare breasted like people might in some remote tribe. If you are too different, other people think you are a little bit wacky and crazy, and most of us would rather not have those labels. Put simply, we become conditioned by our environment, and it happens without us being consciously aware of it. Daring to be different takes real courage, it means breaking free from the herd of humanity around you. It is true you might fail, you might be wrong, but ultimately, it is people who dare to be different, who end up making the greatest difference, and achieving extraordinary things, not ordinary things. To begin with, it can make you feel exposed, it can open you up to ridicule, criticism or worse. There are countless famous people who were painfully rejected before making it big including: Walt Disney, Madonna, Elvis, JK Rowling, Steve Jobs, Lady Gaga, Albert Einstein, Charles Darwin, Isaac Newton, Socrates, Abraham Lincoln, Vincent Van Goch, Steven Spielberg, Michael Jordan, and Rudyard Kipling.

Remember that whether you think you can, or whether you think you can't do something; you are likely to be right.

There are an almost infinite number of ways you can see, think and act differently, I'll suggest are some generic ways, but I am sure you will be able to think of specific things relating precisely to your personal situation.

You can be the slow tortoise that beats the fast hare, if you have the courage to see, think, and act differently

The important thing is to use your imagination and to have the courage to dare to be different, and to accept and learn from failure and set backs, which are inevitable. It is better if you are going to fail, to fail fast, learn your lessons and move on. It might seem strange, but celebrating failure has become a big thing in silicon valley, and a trend in TED talks. Learning from others is useful. It can be motivational to discover how the world's most famous, well respected and successful people have overcome failure.

Change how you see thing

There are a number of ways you can see / perceive things differently:

1. *See the bigger picture.*
2. *Dive into the minutia and see things at a greater depth; put things under the microscope.*
3. *See further, by seeing the future and imagining and antic- ipating what might be beyond the horizon, see what could be, or what should be, so you can be ahead of the game.*
4. *See things from other people's perspective, put yourself in their shoes.*
5. *See why you can, not why you can't.*
6. *Change your self-image, and the way you see yourself.*

"Vision can be incredibly powerful."

Change what and how you think

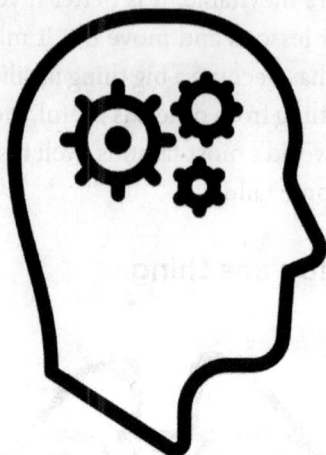

1. Research.
2. Study.
3. Identify leaders and see what they are thinking.
4. Join Dots / Make Connections.
5. Be open minded.
6. Be positive.
7. Look for synergy and win/win / mutual benefit opportunities and interdependence.
8. Question everything.
9. Create hypotheses and seek to consider them and test them out.
10. Use your imagination, and remember that no lesser person than Einstein said "Imagination is more important than knowledge".
11. Think differentiation.
12. Think improvement.
13. Believe in yourself.
14. Believe you can.
15. Believe you will succeed even if it takes you time to do it.

Change what you do

1. *Do different things.*
2. *Do the same things but differently.*
3. *Do more or less of things.*
4. *Be first.*
5. *Be original.*
6. *Be best.*
7. *Practice.*
8. *Be persistent.*
9. *Have a structure and system.*
10. *Be resourceful.*
11. *Try new and different things out and see if they work.*
12. *Raise your standards.*

Changing how you see things, what and how you think, and what you do, in itself isn't enough, because being different usually only works if you are different and better, or offer something new that people want and are prepared to buy, or buy into.

Change can make previously impossible things possible

Richard Branson or Elon Musk may at times appear a little bit wacko, and whilst not everything they do results in success, they direct their energies in ways that have a chance of succeeding. Just remember you have not failed unless you give up, and that success is simply failure turned inside out, and that every failure can be a valuable learning experience.

I recommend you use love, wisdom and imagination as indicators on a compass to guide you. You can rarely achieve great success without the support of others, therefore basing yourself in a caring love energy is likely to be a wise strategy. By love, I am not talking about being all lovey kisses and hugs, although in some circumstances that might work, I am using love in terms of being caring, empathetic, coming from a position of good. Wisdom means trying to be wise, and imagination is the thing that Einstein says is more valuable than knowledge.

The Blain Change Framework™

When George W Bush and Tony Blair, led the invasion of Iraq on the basis that Iraq had weapons of mass destruction that they were just about to use, many thought they were right, but it turned out that they were wrong.

When the bankers came up with wonderful new financial instruments, and made a lot of money, many thought that the banks were great trustworthy businesses, it subsequently transpired that there weren't, they created a financial catastrophe and global recession.

When Hitler rose to power in Germany, the country was in a bad state, and people were demoralised. Many people thought Hitler was good, but it turned out he was one of the evillest people the world has ever seen.

When Nelson Mandela was imprisoned for 27 years, there were many including the United States Government thought he was a bad person, but it turned out that he was a good person, and he went on to win the Nobel Peace Prize, and become president of the Republic of South Africa.

Author JK Rowling, was supposedly turned down by 12 publishers for her Harry Potter book, because they didn't think it would sell, but it went on to become one of the highest selling book series ever.

The pop group the Beetles, were turned down by Decca records who apparently thought guitar groups were falling out of favour, they went on to become one of the world's best-selling groups ever.

When Roger Bannister first ran the four-minute mile, people thought it wasn't possible, but after he did it, lots of others did it too.

In South Africa, and indeed parts of the USA, they thought it was a good thing to racially segregate people, it was clearly never acceptable.

In the UK, at one time, women weren't allowed to vote, and many people thought that was right, it is obviously not right.

Many early seafarers used to think that the world was flat, and that they would be in danger of sailing off the edge of the world, we know now the world is actually round.

For over two thousand years, until the late nineteenth century, a common medical practice called bloodletting was carried out, with the intention of curing or preventing disease, we now know that in all but a very small number of instances it is actually very harmful.

It is easy to look at some of these things in history and be aghast, but every day, pretty much everywhere, there are things that people think that are right, that are wrong, things that people think are good, that are actually bad, things that people think are impossible, that are actually possible, things that people think are unimportant, that are actually important, things that people think are acceptable, that are unacceptable, things that people thing are positive, that are actually negative, things that people think are not urgent, that are actually highly urgent, and things that people believe to be facts, that are actually fiction, and vice versa e.g. the opposite of all these things can be true.

Most people will feel most comfortable doing what everyone else does, on the often wrong assumption, that just because everyone else believes something or does something, that it must be right. Often pioneers, scientists and visionaries who took views contrary to public opinion were ridiculed, held up as heretics, and even killed. Galileo was put under house arrest for supporting the theory that the earth revolved around the sun. When Darwin put forward his scientific theory of natural selection in 1838, he withheld its publication for eight years because of fear of opposition and ridicule. When Louis Pasteur had the audacity to suggest that disease was spread by germs, in the 1850's, he was met with violent resistance from the medical community. Don't make the mistake of thinking that these things couldn't happen today. In psychology there is a term "false consensus" that explains how and why these things happen. You need to think for yourself, and be prepared to continually question everything, and consider all possibilities.

More than ever, we need to embrace wisdom, love and imagination, and continually be challenging ourselves and others, and having opinions on the following eternal conundrums, what is:

Right	Wrong
Good	Bad
Possible	Impossible
Important	Not important
Acceptable	Not Acceptable
Positive	Negative
Urgent	Not Urgent
Fact	Fiction

I call this framework the "Blain Change Framework™". Invariably change and transformation comes when you apply this framework to issues, and make a shift. If you want to achieve something or are facing an issue, start to put your assumptions, thoughts and beliefs through this framework and be prepared to break free from doing what the majority are doing. It takes real courage to leave the herd, and take your own path, but it can feel liberating. The greatest achievements have usually come from those who pioneered, who questioned everything who continually asked themselves: Why? Why not? and What if? People who had the courage of their conviction, who dared to be different and do different things.

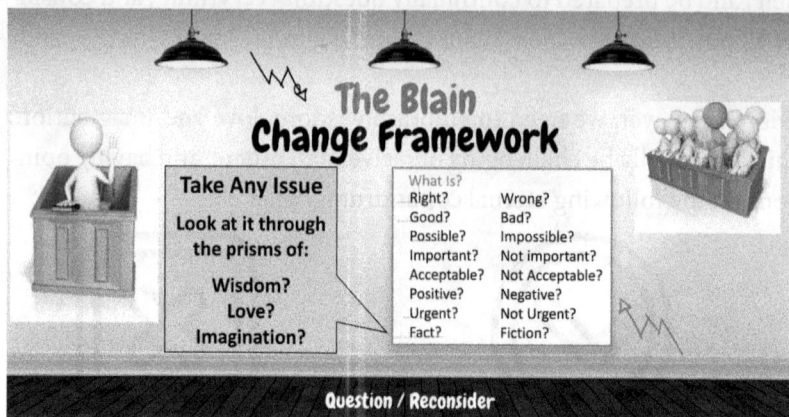

None of us a perfect, we are all completely fallible human beings, we will get things wrong, that is inevitable. There is also often not a clear cut right and wrong; recognising that, can be immensely powerful.

I recall talking to Michael Wilson, one of the most successful business leaders I have met, who co-founded the financial services company St James's Place and helped it grow from a near start up to a FTSE 250 and for a while FTSE 100 company. He told me that he would contemplate major decisions over night, and come up with lists of pros and cons, and also take counsel from people whose opinions he valued and trusted, to help him to make the best decisions.

When the investment bankers were making vast amounts of money, and receiving their huge bonuses, feeling they were masters of the universe, they could point to their success, and it could be difficult to argue against the profit and loss and balance sheet facts, yet what they were doing was as unsustainable as any Ponzi scheme. There is so much uncertainty in the world, it is difficult to know what will happen next. Unlikely, improbable things can and do happen, which can be disconcerting.

You need to bear in mind, that there are often many different ways that results can be achieved, which is best, can depend upon many different factors, like the external circumstances, the people involved, and the timing etc. The truth matters a great deal. Make as wise decisions as you can.

See the big picture and join the dots

See the Big Picture and Connect the Dots

You need to see the big picture as well as the minutiae, regularly ask your self challenging questions about your assumptions, your beliefs, and the evidence. You need to use your imagination to project into the future, and imagine what could be or should be, what might be the likely outcomes of different choices, what might be the best paths, the best ways etc. Try and be wise,make wise choices and take wise action. When you appear to get it right, don't let your ego blind you, try to have humility and recognise that often you need time to really see if things were right in the long run.

Don't beat yourself up if you get it wrong, it is inevitable you will, but try to learn something from every failure, every setback, every mistake, every experience as well as every success. Remember success is rarely permanent and failure is rarely terminal.

The singer Madonna wrote a great children's story book called "The English Roses". The book is about the lives of girls: Charlotte, Amy, Grace and Nicole. They become jealous of a pretty and studious girl called Binah, whose life they believe is perfect. They are jealous of her, and are mean and unfriendly towards her. The truth is, that Binah's mother died when she was young, and she lives with her father in a small house where she cooks, cleans and works very hard. It is a sweet little story, with a nice moral and a happy ending, that the mean girls discover the truth, and all the girls become friends.

This might be a fictional story, but all too often in life, it is easy to jump to the wrong conclusion. Often the clues to the truth are there, it is just that we don't join the dots, and see the bigger picture, or even if we do see the bigger picture, we don't change our beliefs and actions as a result. You have to have the mindset of a detective, with an alertness and awareness. You've got to look for connections, often the greatest scientific breakthroughs and discoveries come from scientists seeing the connections between things. It is only when you truly see the big picture of your life, that you can join the dots, and discover how connected and intertwined your career is with your life. Seeing the bigger picture, enables you to understand where you are in your life, how much time you might have left, and the insight into what is important and what isn't, and ultimately what is most important.

If you see the bigger picture and join the dots you can reduce risks and create great opportunities. In the last financial crash Warren Burret reportedly made $10billion plus, buying cheap stock when others lost confidence and fortunes. Apple were able to see the big picture and the join the dots when they invented the iPhone. Kodak, who invented digital photography were not, and ended up filing for bankruptcy. If you see the bigger picture and join the dots you will realise that large number of jobs and professions are at high risk of automisation in the next 20 years.

When you see the bigger picture and join the dots, you will discover the world and humanity are on the edge of crises that threaten our survival.

CHAPTER 2

LIVING IN AN UNPRECEDENTED TIME IN HUMAN HISTORY

"Once you realise that we are living in the most extraordinary period in the 50,000 years that modern man, (Homo Sapiens) have existed, you start to realise why we are facing as many challenges as we are."

If there was a painting of you in your life, there would be a picture of you in the middle and world you live in around you. Your life experience is heavily influenced by the world around you, and everything within it. Whilst it is natural to see ourselves as separate from the world, we are actually as much part of it, as it is part of us. You'd appear in other people's paintings. What is going on the world can and frequently does impact us.

The first thing you need to understand, is that three hugely significant things have happened, or factors have come together, that means we are living in an unprecedented time in human history, which is the reason that we need a radical new approach to the way we live our lives and manage our careers. These three things are:

1. A time of exponential progress and change.

2. A global population explosion.

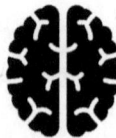

3. An exponential growth in knowledge.

Joseph Blain, Author's Grandfather, Born 1865

These are not small insignificant things, they are huge issues and massively significant, and they need to be recognised. Because we are here, living on earth right now, the status quo is our normal, but in human history and evolution terms, it is not normal at all, it is truly extraordinary.

To put these things into context, I'd like to share some of my family history. It might be unusual in that my grandfather was seventy when my dad was conceived, which means he was born in 1865. At the time of writing this book, it was announced in the newspapers that 72-year-old Rolling Stone, Sir Mick Jagger, is expecting his eighth baby, which shows it is possible!

I.   Exponential Rate of Progress and Change

When my grandfather was born, author Charles Dickens was still alive, it was a time before, the Wright Brothers and the first powered flight, before motor cars with internal combustion engines, before electricity, before telephones, before wireless communication, and obviously well before things like computers, the internet and social media etc.

In just three generations of my family, the world has changed beyond all belief; mankind has put men on the moon, sent probes to distant planets, put satellites in space, that enable us to navigate with GPS with precision, and communicate with each other easily.

Every day, there are supposedly a city of a million people in the air, in jet airliners, crisscrossing the globe at 20,000 ft. + altitude, travelling at 400mph+ in comfort. We are living in the information age, and a time of unprecedented scientific and engineering breakthroughs. With fibre optic networks, we can communicate at the speed of light; mobile and internet technologies connect us together in ways that could hardly have previously been imagined. We've got smart phones, personal computers, super computers and so much more. We've got the technology and ability to do extraordinary things, like curing diseases, transplanting human organs like hearts, from dead people, to living people. We've even been able to map the human genome, which has given us the ability, for the first time, to read nature's complete genetic blueprint for building a human being.

THE STARTING POINT.....

Things are changing so fast we hardly know what will happen tomorrow, let alone next year. Many people starting University now, may find themselves in new jobs that haven't yet been invented. Things that we have never heard of, can quickly become a part of our lives. Facebook for example was only founded in 2004, but at the time of writing this book it has approx. 1.65 billion active monthly users, and is valued at $350 billion. Google was only founded in 1998, and at the time of writing this book, its parent company Alphabet, was valued at about $570 billion. Today it is difficult to imagine a world without Google, smart phones, the internet, and all the technology we have come to rely on.

2.   Global Population Explosion

When my grandfather was born, the population of the world was approximately 1.2 billion, when dad was born it was about 2 billion, when I was born in 1963 it was approx. 3.4 billion and now it is now 7.4 billion and rising fast. At the time this book was written, it was predicted that the global population will rise to 9.7 billion by 2050. Just think of the impact of that population growth on the world's natural resources and the environment, and the competition for land and resources? Since mankind started to explore the whole world, it must originally have seemed such a vast place with an abundance of resources, but now we are beginning to realise that mankind is having a huge impact on the natural world, and most of it, is not a good impact.

According to the Population Reference Bureau in the USA, since Homo Sapiens arrived about 50,000 years ago, about 107 billion people (modern humans) have lived in the world, that means that there would be approximately 15 dead people, for every single person alive today, which doesn't seem very many to me.

The global population growth in the last two hundred years is stagger-ing, with the last hundred years being the most extraordinary. The last 100 years represents just 0.002% of the time that human beings have existed.

The global population of human beings seems normal to us today, but in the history of humanity, it is the complete opposite of normal. Not only are the resources in our world having to support six times as many people as they did when my grandfather was born, the use of those resources per person, has increased massively, as life in the modern world is based upon having vast quantities of stuff, which re-quires vast quantities of natural resources. In recent years', sustainabil-ity has become an issue that many are aware of, yet sustainability in context of use of natural resources, still seems like a drop in the ocean in terms of what is needed, given that consumption appears to be ris-ing dramatically, particularly as vast numbers of people in developing countries, start to replicate the lifestyles of developed countries.

The biggest threat to humanity, is humanity itself. With technology of the modern world, our capacity to do harm to each other and the planet has never been greater. Out of the 7.4 billion people alive, it is probably possible for just two people only to destroy humanity com-pletely e.g. if the Presidents of the USA and Russia pressed the but-tons on their entire nuclear bomb arsenals. Biological weapons could probably do a similar thing.

What is perhaps scarier, and perhaps more likely, is that we 7.4 bil-lion humans will individually do things that cause great harm without even realising what we are doing; global warming is just one example of this, with the burning of fossil fuels, and other man made activity being responsible for changing the climate of the world.

When 7.4 billion people change their habits, it can have a massive im-pact positively or negatively. The more connected the world is, the more likely it is that people will change their habits. The biggest technology companies are looking into ways that they can bring low cost broadband to virtually the entire population of the world. Facebook are busy building giant solar powered drones that can stay airborne for months at a time to provide broadband to remote areas, Elon Musk is looking at building a constellation of low cost satellites to do the same, and Google have Project Loon, which is exploring the possibility of having high altitude helium balloons in the stratosphere to provide internet access to remote rural locations. Microsoft has launched a 4Afrika Initiative to bring Internet access to low-income residents of Africa. I don't think these companies are doing these things out of pure altruism, I think they are going to want to make money from them also.

Whilst technology can be used by the world's population that have access to it, for greater good, it can also be used to achieve great harm, whether it is an epidemic of cyber bullying, that can affect people of almost all ages, the loss of human to human interaction, or the enablement of criminal organisations, paedophiles and terrorist networks, who are hell bent on bringing evil ideologies, death and destruction to the world.

The inequalities within the population of the world are staggering; can you imagine the impact of the most deprived in the world, being given access the internet, which enables them to see the inequality and do little about it. Whilst it could reduce inequality, if it goes badly, it could drive migration on a global scale, and create wars and violence over resources. It needs to be managed with positive global strategies, driven to support equality, harmony and fairness. We've seen how the terrorist group ISIS has been made possible by technology and the super connected world. The underworld and criminal gangs have been quick to embrace cybercrime and to use the Dark Web for dark things. Things can change so fast that we never know what might happen next.

A large growing global population presents challenges that mankind has never faced before; they are challenges we'd be foolish to ignore.

3. Exponential Growth in Knowledge

Buckminster Fuller, was an author, visionary and futurist, he created the "Knowledge Doubling Curve". He deduced that until 1900, human knowledge doubled approximately once a century, by the end of WWII, it had reduced to doubling every 25 years. With the internet and modern technology, knowledge is thought to be doubling every 12 months, and according to IBM, the arrival and growth of the "Internet of Things", will lead to a doubling of knowledge every 12 hours.

Knowledge used to be available only to the few, now it is available to the many.

Knowledge used to be available only to the few, now it is available to the many. The ever increasing amount of knowledge is staggering, but the quantity of knowledge is so great, it is difficult to see the wood for the trees, to know what is important knowledge and what isn't; we are continually fighting information overload. There is so much knowledge to know, it is simply overwhelming, no longer can we hope to retain all the important knowledge in our brains, we just need to know how to access it.

Knowledge Growth With Curve

With Internet of Things IBM Predict
Knowledge Might Soon Doubled Every 12 Hours

Now Knowledge Doubles Once Per Year

Increase in Knowledge

Until 1900 - Knowledge Doubbles Once Per Century

Exponential
Growth

Time   © Jonathan Blain 2015

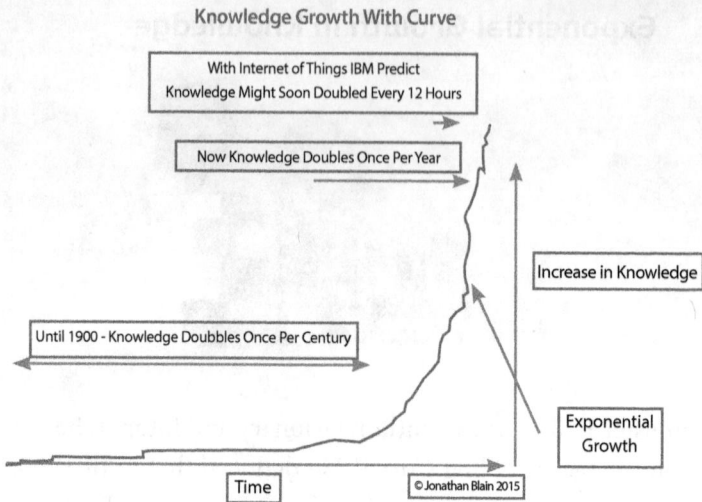

We also have an irksome problem, in that some of the knowledge we have is wrong, either because it was never right in the first place, or because circumstances have changed. Increasingly we need to be able to unlearn things that are no longer relevant or true. We can only retain so much information in our brains, so it is vitally important that we retain the most important and useful knowledge. I was talking to my mother who is edging towards 80, and she was telling me some of the issues she was having to deal with, bombarded by emails and communications from banks, having to sift through messages to identify what was phishing and what was real. Her broadband provider had put her onto a new plan that she hadn't agreed to, assigning her automatically to services that she didn't want or even know what they are. She has been bamboozled, she has had to learn about computing, the internet, emails and security protocols, things that never existed when she was a child. Even getting into modern cars can seem bewildering with car computers, different modes and functions, it all requires knowledge that a generation ago you didn't need.

We are all faced with the possibility that we could make profoundly important life and career decisions, based on knowledge that is wrong now, or may become wrong in the future. How many times are we told things are good for us by experts, such as doctors or politicians, only to be told in the future that they were not good for us at all, in fact they were positively harmful. I remember when we were told that diesel cars were highly fuel efficient and were good for the environment, now we are told their emissions are very bad for us and the environment. It is estimated that 50,000 people die every year in the UK with conditions linked to polluted air, and according to The World Health Organisation, air pollution is leading to as many as three million premature deaths every year worldwide. Particles of pollution have been found in people's brains and scientists are questioning whether it might be responsible for an upsurge in Alzheimer's disease.

I remember my dad telling me a story of when he went to visit his mother's doctor, when she was dying a nasty painful death from lung cancer. He instinctively offered the doctor a cigarette, because almost everyone smoked, and that was the first time that he learnt that smoking had anything to do with lung cancer. He never smoked another cigarette again.

It is not just that we as humanity can get small things wrong, we can also get big things wrong too. Few people thought there was anything fundamentally wrong with the global financial systems and practices of bankers, but we know now that there was, which resulted in the global financial crisis in 2007 / 2008, the effects of which are still being felt today. What is incredible, is how a few decisions of just a few people, can have profoundly positive or negative impacts on the many.

We didn't know there was anything wrong with burning fossil fuels, until we discovered global warming, which

Mankind is responsible for vast toxic pollution

is changing the world's climate, causing weather extremes, including droughts, floods and storms. Crops are failing, lands that were previously habitable are becoming inhabitable, the ice caps are melting, sea levels are rising, and the consequences are the death of some people, and the possibility of mass migrations on a scale that is almost unimaginable. We thought asbestos was good and used it everywhere, until we discovered it was extremely dangerous and killed people. Life in the modern world has got so complex, that we need vast amounts of knowledge simply to be able to function and do even basic things.

Today in context of evolution

Most of us, got to learn about Darwin and the theory of evolution at school. The concept is that over time, biological things e.g. animals and plants change, evolve, or become extinct and cease to exist at all. We are all aware that dinosaurs went extinct, but every year there are many species that are thought to go extinct.

"According to the UN Environment Programme, the Earth is in the midst of a mass extinction of life. Scientists estimate that 150-200 species of plant, insect, bird and mammal become extinct every 24 hours. This is nearly 1,000 times the "natural" or "background" rate and, say many biologists, is greater than anything the world has experienced since the vanishing of the dinosaurs nearly 65m years ago. Around 15% of mammal species and 11% of bird species are classified as threatened with extinction".
Source – Guardian Newspaper

It would appear that this is largely mankind's fault.

If we are not an animal or nature lover, we might not care about these extinctions, until you start to think deeply about the consequences and implications to humanity and all living things on earth. Until I researched these facts, I was completely unaware of these extinctions, and to be honest, I was totally shocked, seriously alarmed and concerned.

It is easy to find yourself living in a bubble without realising it.

One thing I have observed, is that life is so hard for so many people, that looking after yourself and your family, takes pretty much all your effort; it is like we are all in our own little bubbles, separated from many of the bigger issues that are going on around us. As a result, it is difficult to put much energy or thought into issues for humanity as a whole. I think most people feel that there is someone, somewhere taking care of all the things they can't take care of. I am concerned that this isn't always the case, and that those who have taken up the mantle of caring like politicians, don't always fully understand the issues, sometimes have vested interests that aren't for a greater good, or they unintentionally don't make wise choices. I believe politicians are hugely important, they do very difficult jobs, and if we think we could do better, we should do so, not criticise them.

It is not that world leaders don't know about hugely important issues regarding the future of humanity, the United Nations has many reports that say it how it is. They simply either choose to ignore the longer term issues in favour of short term priorities, or they don't believe the scientists, or they don't care, or they can't agree to collectively make decisions or take actions. I accept it is hard to be a politician and they need understanding.

Even when they make commitments, they often fail to implement them. An election can change who is in power, and then everything changes. US President Donald Trump, said before he was elected in 2016, that he wants to start resuming coal mining, and keep heavily polluting power stations which burn fossil fuels, because he doesn't believe climate change. This was said just before the USA made a commitment to ratify to Paris Climate Accord, which seeks to reduce harmful greenhouse gas emissions that cause climate change, which is seen as essential by most scientists to avoid a global catastrophe. Politics is like "Mission Impossible" at times.

It is remarkably easy to mix up what is right and wrong

I've observed that in the modern world, there appears to be a conflict between humanity doing what is morally and philosophically right, and what makes money. All too often, I think the drive for profit, normally seems to win. In Davos in 2016, it was reported that the richest 1% had more wealth that than the other 99%. I don't know what you think, but seems wrong to me? With money comes a lot of power and influence, and I fear that those with the money care more about themselves and their money, than they do for the other 99% and for a greater good of humanity. Edmund Burke said "The only thing necessary for the triumph of evil is for good men to do nothing". Surely wrecking our planet, spoiling the future of our children if we have any, and future generations, has to be classed as evil? Are we all unwittingly party to the biggest man made destruction of our planet in human history? Is the status quo in the world acceptable? Are we on the right path for a better future, or are we still on the wrong path? I think the answer to these questions is we are still collectively on the wrong path, but you can make up your own mind. You only need to look at history to see that mankind is capable of some pretty horrific things, and it is not all in some distant past. You only need to look back over the past 100 years to see countless horrors of two world wars, genocides, the use of nuclear bombs, environmental catastrophe's, entire states collapsing with anarchy unfolding, mass migration, terrible diseases like Ebola, and a rise in horrific terrorist atrocities. I believe lots of us feel powerless to do anything about these issues; alone we can't solve all the world problems, but we can positively impact our own world. If lots of people do that, it has a ripple effect into the wider world, and that is when incredibly positive things become possible. Wouldn't that be amazing?

It has to be wrong that the richest 1% are richer than the other 99%

FAT CAT
FLAP

The distribution of wealth in the world is a big problem

At the time of writing this book, there was a furore going on in the UK, over the collapse of a retail store group called BHS, which is where I had my first part time job, whilst still at school. The BBC reported that a British billionaire entrepreneur called Sir Phillip Green, extracted large amounts of money from the business, before selling it for a pound to someone else, after which the business collapsed with the loss of approx. 11,000 jobs and a £571m deficit in the company's pension fund.

"A damning MPs' report found Sir Philip, the billionaire former owner of BHS, extracted large sums and left the business on "life support".
Source BBC

At nearly the same time, Sir Phillip Green took delivery of his new 295ft super yacht ship, which is valued at $150m. The media were chasing him in his ship around the Greek Islands, asking for an interview. I don't know Sir Philip Green, and I know there are always two sides to everything, but from the outside it appears that one person has amassed enormous wealth at the expense of thousands of ordinary innocent people, who've lost their jobs and their pension income. There is no suggestion that Sir Philip Green has done anything illegal, and he is saying he is going to do something voluntarily about the pension deficit, but the situation illustrates the inequality in the world, and how it is possible for a few people, to be able to inflict devastating consequences on the masses. I wonder how Sir Philip feels being pilloried by the media and the British parliament? Has his 295ft motor yacht and his billionaire lifestyle, put him and his family in a gilded cage? How would you feel if you were in Sir Philip's situation? Is the price of extreme success really worth it?

Money buys influence and access to power, and it is often said that power corrupts. It is not hard to conceive that those with the deepest pockets, will be able to make the right connections, lobby and influence those in power, to adopt policies and make decisions that are beneficial to them. Often what is best for the privileged few, is not best for the many. Politicians are in somewhat of a nightmare situation, where they need the support of those with money to get elected, and also need those with money to invest, and to do so in a way that will create jobs and wealth for the ordinary people too. I am not for a moment suggesting that the richest 1% are all bad, but I believe it is morally and socially wrong to have such a wealth imbalance in the world. I commend billionaires like Bill Gates and Warren Buffet and others who have committed to giving away most of their money, in a way that makes the greatest difference to humanity.

As the population of the world grows exponentially, at the same time as mankind's ability to cause harm to the planet and to each other, it can be of little surprise that there is huge uncertainty, and as many threats, as there are opportunities.

Every year, little lion cubs born on the savanna in Africa, grow up just like their parents did, they learn to hunt and feed and reproduce, just like lions have probably done for thousands of years. They live like nature intended them to. Every year, migratory birds will go on their migrations, humpback whales will make their way towards their migratory destinations like Silver Bank off the Dominican Republic; animal species seem to know what to do.

No other species other than humans, grows up wondering what it will be when it grows up, yet we human beings have almost infinite choices, and choices frequently equal pressure and stress, and they can have either positive or negative consequences. Are we going to be a doctor, a nurse, an engineer, a scientist, a teacher, a farmer, a fisherman, a pilot, a soldier, a politician etc. According to a Study by Oxford University and Deloitte, 35% of jobs today are at high risk of computerisation in the next 20 years, are you in one of these, or planning to go into one of these careers?

Many careers are already in decline, jobs that we once thought were secure, are turning out to be anything but secure, and many people are needing multiple careers in their lifetime, not just multiple jobs.

We've just got a new kitten. I was watching it today playing, getting into all its cute little kitten behaviours, learning to climb, jump and hunt all on its own through play. I wonder how it learnt to use its cat litter and not do its stuff all over the floor or furniture? I was thinking how it has arrived in the world, instinctively knowing how to be a cat. We've also got an older cat, that we had from a kitten, it regularly goes out on adventures, it is forever crossing the road, and touch wood, it seems to know how to avoid running out under the wheels of a car. I remember when my children were young, teaching them to cross the road, making sure they were safe, but you can't teach a cat the green cross code!

We arrive in this world as a result of a biological code that determines so much about us. What chance does that biological code have of adapting us to the challenges and opportunities we face today? In a way we are genuinely connected to all living organisms, in that we store genetic information using the same molecules: DNA and RNA. Within genetic code of these molecules is compelling evidence of the shared ancestry of all living things.

Genes are discrete sections of the DNA sequence, which provide the biochemical instructions for producing all of the components of biological organisms. As human beings, we have all the core parts of our bodies, but some parts of us, like the shape of our face, our size, our appearance and other features are unique because of small variations.

Gene Facts

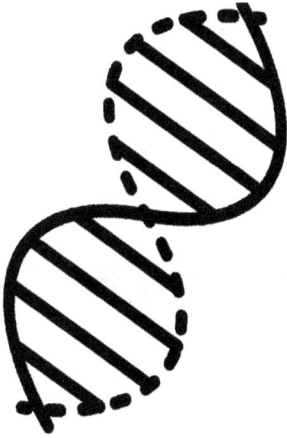

- 100% of humans have the same genes, but the sequence difference makes each person unique.
- Our genes are 98% similar to chimpanzees.
- Our genes are 92% similar to most mammals including mice.
- 44% of our genes are similar to insects including fruit flies.
- 26% of our genes are similar to single cell organisms including yeast.
- 18% of our genes are similar to plants.

Through our DNA and Genes, we are connected to all living things; we are collectively part of a universal whole of life. There is an interdependence between life forms, where we actually need the other parts. Plants are for example the only organisms that can convert light energy from the sun into food. Put simply: no plants = no animals and no us. It is not just food that plants make, it is oxygen as well, that we and all living things need to live: no oxygen = no life. Plants also provide habitats in which we and other animals can live, without plant based habitats, the earth would be like the moon. Plants make and preserve soil, so that other plants can grow, they also beautify the world. Are you beginning to join the dots?

As a species, we human beings seem so different, we are completely dependent upon our parents or adult carers for years, we are like plasticine modelling clay, in that our lives can be moulded into so many different shapes. Each of us has so much potential, and often so many choices, yet at the same time, I believe we have a common humanity inside us, that connects us to each other, regardless of our differences. Whilst we are all so different, there are parts of us that are the same, it is something I'll be coming back to later in this book. The issue of what it means to be human, and what the meaning and purpose behind our lives is, is an essential topic that will be covered later on.

Mankind have become rulers of the world

I believe that being a human being is a privilege. We humans have evolved as rulers and masters of the world, with immense power over our planet and everything within it, including all living things. I think we have a duty and responsibility to be wise and just rulers, and should see ourselves as custodians, not destroyers of our world. Our legacy to future generations, should be a good one, not a bad one, and each of us, needs to shoulder our portion of responsibility. We are all a part of humanity and this is our watch. Your voice, your thoughts, and your actions matter. Evolution is alive today, we have to adapt, and for the better, not the worse.

Have lessons from older times been lost?

Because my wife Jenny has worked in childcare all her adult life, and for the last 25 years has owned and run one of the UK's top Montessori Nursery

Schools, I developed a big interest in child development and education. I've learnt that so much of who we are as adults, was shaped by our early year's experiences. I once picked up and read one of my wife's books called The Continuum Concept, which was written by the late Jean Liedloff.

She went on a number of expeditions deep into the rain forest in Venezuela, spending two and a half years living with remote indigenous tribes. The essence of the book is that: "the continuum concept is the idea, that in order to achieve optimal physical, mental and emotional development, human beings, especially babies, require the kind of experience to which our species adapted during the long process of our evolution". That evolutionary continuum was lost as mankind moved into the modern world, and the consequence is that many of the problems we have today in modern life, don't exist in these remote tribes.

It can be argued, that for all the advances and advantages we have in the modern world, there is also a downside to modern life, we might know more, have more, can do more, but we are not necessarily wiser, happier or more fulfilled. In the modern world, we have become largely disconnected from the natural world, and don't realise how much our lives and the lives of future generations depend upon it, and that is a big problem.

Life has become exponentially more complex. Indigenous people know where their food comes from, but in the modern world, we tend to mostly think that food comes in packets and packages from the supermarket. Look at the ingredients of many foods today, and you are likely to see a mass of chemical additives to make them last longer, and look and taste better etc. In this respect, it looks like a large amount of our food comes from science labs and industrial processes, we've mostly no idea where all these additives come from, what they do, and even whether they are good for us, we just consume without knowing, and trust that someone we don't know, will be responsible and make sure they are safe.

Are the young beginning to know more about the world than the old?

In evolutionary terms, the rate of change, the massive population growth, and the explosion of knowledge is extraordinary; the rules are being rewritten. The lives that many of us are living, are vastly different to the lives our parents led when they were our age, let alone our grandparents.

In generations past, parents would be able to pass on wisdom to their children, who would pass it on to their children, but that continuum has stopped for so many people.

Young children pick up new technology easier than their grandparents

Many toddlers know more about technology than their parents and grandparents. Every day you can go to sleep and wake up, and something major in the world has changed. Collectively, we have never had more, known more, and been able to do more, yet at an individual level, most people at some time will be negatively impacted by the changes.

Whilst many parents are urging their children to work hard at their schoolwork, some teenagers are earning more than their parents have earnt in their lifetime as YouTubers; making videos of their lives, attracting in some cases millions of followers and vast amounts of commercial sponsorship. Some children criticised for playing too many computer games, are finding they can earn a living, and in some cases more than their parents, travelling the world as professional gamers.

University drop outs have been able to become billionaires with start-up technology companies. Are governments, parents and teachers ahead of the game enough, to know how to prepare children for adult life in tomorrow's brave new world? I know these are rhetorical questions, but they are questions that I feel we need to consider. Whatever we think the rules of the game of life are, we need to be prepared to regularly tear them up and rewrite them. Evolution is not just about biology and physiology, it is a word that describes a process of slow change and development, that can relate to anything. Montessori Education is good at preparing children for a changing world.

The changes in the modern world, in terms of progress, population and in knowledge, are anything but slow, they are the absolute opposite; it is like the equivalent of evolution on steroids. Many people see evolution as encompassing society and politics also. I believe that it is hardly surprising that so many people are not OK, mentally, physically, emotionally, and financially etc. If these three things were the only issues, it would be challenging enough, but they are not, there are many other problems in the world, that have the potential to impact all of us.

The balance of opportunity versus threats in the modern world

Imagine a balance with positive things and one side and negative things on the other. On the one hand, we are living at arguably the most exciting time in human history, where extraordinary things are possible, but on the other, the world is literally on the edge of crisis in five principle areas:

1. Economically
2. Politically
3. Socially
4. Environmentally
5. Individually

On the positive side, it could be argued that the human race in the modern western world, has never been wealthier, healthier, safer, freer, better fed and educated. 60 million people were killed in the second world war. Today, we have more, know more, are able to do more, and we live longer than in generations past. A couple of centuries ago, half the British population lived in what would now be classed as extreme poverty. Infant mortality used to be high, and now it is low,

many diseases that would have previously killed us, can now be easily cured with antibiotics, and become nothing more than a temporary inconvenience. In the 1830's in western Europe, life expectancy was just 33, and it has been reported that before 1800, there was not a country in the world with life expectancy of greater than 40. Now an increasing number of people are living to 100, and the life expectancy in the modern world is generally increasing. Despite the rise of terrorism in Europe, deaths from terrorism still remain low. In overall terms; you have a far greater chance of dying due to other causes.

Whether it is good things or bad things, the state of the wider world, is likely to have a big impact on you, and the quality of your own life, and therefore it is something you need to consider.

I am an instinctive optimist; one of my five core strengths on the Clifton Strengths Finder, is positivity, and I believe that we should all be grateful for all the incredible things about living today, but I truly believe that there are major problems in the world, that threaten the very survival of the human race and all living things, and at an individual level, there are also many problems that need solving. I think we would be crazy to ignore reality, and the things that are going on to us and around us.

I am quite frankly alarmed by the state of the world; if the world had warning alarm bells, I think they would be going off right now. I know I am not alone in having concerns. One of the greatest minds of our age, Professor Stephen Hawking said:

"In a world that is in chaos politically, socially and environmentally, how can the human race sustain another 100 years?", later clarifying: "I don't know the answer. That is why I asked the question, to get people to think about it, and to be aware of the dangers we now face."
Professor Stephen Hawking (Source Wikipedia)

Economic Issues

Social Issues

Political Issues   Individual Issues

Environmental
Issues

The Good Ship Opportunity

Economic Issues

The 2007 / 2008 meltdown in global financial systems, and near financial catastrophe that resulted in a global recession, reminds us all of what an interconnected world we now live in. It has been often said, that if America sneezes, the rest of the world catches a cold, but now we know, economic events in China or any major country, can negatively or positively affect the rest of the world.

The world appears to be floating on an ever increasing mountain of debt. We like to think that each generation can have a higher standard of living than the one that preceded it, and the only way it of that happening in many countries, or even the illusion of that happening, appears to be to turn to debt, both national debt, commercial debt and private debt. In 2015, the USA had a Government debt as a percent of GDP of 104.17%, which compares against a record high of 121.70 percent in 1946 after the second world war, and a record low of 31.70 percent in 1974.

In many modern western countries, the population is aging, which means a taxpaying burden will increasingly have to be borne by a relatively smaller percentage of younger age working people, which is not fair.

When economies are struggling as many are now, debt is seen as the only way of keeping Governments, Organisations and Individuals spending. If these groups are not spending, then it costs jobs, and reduces the GDP, which reduces tax revenues.

Debt can solve the problems for a while, but if the debt gets bigger and bigger, eventually it becomes impossible to repay, by individuals, governments or organisations, and that is when financial systems can collapse. There are many countries like Greece, where the financial systems have only been prevented from collapsing by large international bail outs. In 2015, the UK's Telegraph Newspaper suggested "the world economy stands on the brink of a second credit crisis", with a McKinsey & Co study revealing "the staggering scale of the problem as global debt has ballooned by $57 trillion since 2007 to reach about $200 trillion".

There appears no easy solution and no quick solution, the problems could take a generation or more to resolve, and that doesn't seem palatable if it is occurring during your lifetime. Governments and Bankers do not want to alarm us and cause panic, but if you search Google and see the comments that world leaders, central bankers and experts have made, it has to be concerning.

Economic issues can sometimes seem like they are external to us, and don't affect us that much, but times of economic austerity and global recessions, even possibly depressions in recent times, have demonstrated graphically, that economic problems can destroy lives of ordinary people just like us. People can lose their jobs and income, their safety and security, the ability to provide for themselves and their family almost over night.

Political Issues

Politically there are disputes, disagreements, conflicts, wars, genocides, terrorism, dictatorships, migration, lack of judgement and lack of wisdom all over the world. Entire States and officials of some states, are responsible for corruption on a massive scale, and a wide range of ghastly atrocities, including: genocide, ethnic cleansing, persecution, torture, terrorism promotion, murdering people to transplant and sell their organs called "organ harvesting".

Bad governance, bad decisions and short termism, can have hugely negative impacts, with long term consequences. These issues can occur at local, national and international levels. The United Nations is struggling to cope with an overwhelming number of incredibly important issues all over the world. They are short of staff, short of money and resources, and short of support from sovereign nations, many of whom are the cause of the problems. Many countries rulers are ruthless dictators, running countries as their personal fiefdoms, others are elected but act as dictators.

There are huge political issues and challenges around the world at every level. We need incredibly wise politicians more than ever before, and they seem in very short supply.

Social Issues

Socially, there are an abundance of problems including: social care, crime, corruption, persecution, addictions, racism, hatred, discrimination, inequality, poverty and depravation, cruelty, bullying including online bullying / trolling, revenge pornography, shame blackmail, domestic violence and abuse, knife and gun crime, anti-social behaviour, and all sorts of other despicable things like slavery, people trafficking, female genital mutilation, sexism, misogyny and pedophilia. People are living longer, which is putting strain on health services, and social care costs. Unhealthy lifestyles are causing other health problems like obesity and diabetes. The list of important social issues goes on and on.

Environmental Issues

Environmentally, the world is totally on the edge, man-made activities has caused pollution that has affected the climate of the world, causing global warming that is resulting in floods and droughts, which has resulted in failure of crops and famines, and many natural disasters. Ice caps are melting, sea levels are rising, and parts of the world currently habitable, are set to become inhabitable. and people are dying. A few extra degrees in temperature doesn't seem like a big thing, until you learn that it is putting hundreds of millions of lives and risk, and could easily become the cause of mass death and migrations, social unrest, wars, economic disasters and extinction of many entire species, including possibly us. There is a saying, when you are in a hole stop digging, but humanity hasn't stopped digging, things are getting worse. Whilst climate agreements have been signed and initiatives put in place to improve things, everything seems too little too late. Doing something is better than nothing, but it is clearly not enough.

Mankind has helped itself to the world's natural resources like the fossil fuels, oil and gas, and to everything: forests, oceans, minerals and metals etc. without realising that many of those resources are finite, and without realising there can be negative consequences. We've used chemicals on the land, that have been carried by waterways into the seas, killing life in the oceans and for much of the time, we've not even been aware of what we are doing. We have polluted the seas with plastic and other things, and have over-fished species to near extinction, without realising that we depend upon the ocean to sustain our lives and all living things. We've done stupid thing, like putting tiny microbeads of plastic into cosmetics, tooth paste, body washes, cleaning products and other things, which according to the UK Environment Minister Andrea Leadsom, is "causing irreversible damage to the environment, with billions of indigestible plastic pieces poisoning sea creatures".

We can be in awe of all the positive things that mankind has done, but we can also be alarmed by all the negative things we have collectively done in the past, and are still doing today. We are not just plundering the planets natural resources, we are polluting it too; our man made activities are changing nature itself.

The environment is in crisis and five of the biggest issues are:

1. Mankind is destroying the oceans and marine life.
2. Human activity is changing the climate in the world.
3. Mankind is responsible for the biggest mass extinction since the loss of dinosaurs.
4. Our diet is a major contributor to climate change.
5. A tenth of the world's wildernesses has disappeared in the last 20 years.

The status quo is strange, in that in the modern western world, we are collectively responsible, yet we don't typically feel individually responsible, and don't recognise that the choices and actions we personally make impact the world. If we all made changes we could solve collective problems; we need to be the change we want and need.

① 1

Manking destroying the oceans and marine life

Arguably the world's greatest ever ocean researcher, Sylvia Earle, said in her TED Talk, that in the last 50 years, mankind has eaten 90% of the big fish in the oceans, destroyed over half the coral in the world, and have been responsible for a large depletion of oxygen in large areas of the Pacific, which should not just be a concern for the animals that are dying, but for all of us as well. Sylvia Earle was born in 1935, she has been a National Geographic explorer-in-residence since 1998. She was the first female chief scientist of the U.S. National Oceanic and Atmospheric Administration, and was named by Time Magazine as its first Hero for the Planet in 1998.

> "I'm haunted by the thought of what Ray Anderson calls "tomorrow's child," asking why we didn't do something on our watch to save sharks and blue fin tuna, and squids, and coral reefs, and the living ocean, while there still was time. Well, now is that time. I hope for your help, to explore and protect the wild ocean in ways that will restore its health, and in so doing, secure hope for humankind. Health to the ocean means health for us…. And I hope that someday we will find evidence that there is intelligent life among humans on this planet". Sylvia Earle

┌───┐
│ ② │
│ Human activity changing the climate of the world │
└───┘

Ex US Vice President Al Gore, has become a champion of climate change issues, he wrote a book and helped create a film titled: "The Inconvenient Truth", which he uses to explain how mankind's activities are having a dramatic effect of the world's climate, and it is already having a dramatic impact on humanity and all living things, and could have profound negative implications for all life on earth. His premise is that a commonly held belief is that: "The Earth is so big, we can't possibly have any lasting, harmful impact on the Earth's environment". The truth is that we can, and we are.

Climate change has become a big issue for humanity, but twenty or thirty years before this book was written, it wasn't something that ordinary people really thought or worried about, let alone Governments and World Leaders.

(3)

> Mankind responsible for   the biggest mass extinctions since the Dinosaurs

"The Earth has lost half of its wildlife in the past 40 years." World Wildlife Fund

Man made activity isn't just changing the climate, polluting the land and the oceans, killing off life in the oceans, it is responsible for arguably the biggest mass extinction since the loss of the Dinosaurs nearly 65 million years ago.

The secretary-general of the UN Convention on Biological Diversity, Ahmed Djoghlaf said, before leaving his post:

"Nations risk economic collapse and loss of culture, if it does not protect the natural world... What we are seeing today is a total disaster..... No country has met its targets to protect nature. We are losing biodiversity at an unprecedented rate.
If current levels [of destruction] go on, we will reach a tipping point very soon. The future of the planet now depends on governments taking action in the next few years...... Industrialisation, population growth, the spread of cities and farms and climate change are all now threatening the fundamentals of life itself".

"The Earth is in the midst of a mass extinction of life. Scientists estimate that 150-200 species of plant, insect, bird and mammal become extinct every 24 hours. This is nearly 1,000 times the "natural" or "background" rate and, say many biologists, is greater than anything the world has experienced since the vanishing of the dinosaurs nearly 65m years ago. Around 15% of mammal species and 11% of bird species are classified as threatened with extinction".
UN Environment Programme

Stanford University Professor, Paul Ehrlich, co-author of the Science Advances study said: "Biodiversity is essential for human health, economies, food production and cultures. There are examples of species all over the world that are essentially the walking dead. We're sawing off the limb that we are sitting on". Mark Urban and ecologist at the University of Connecticut reviewed 131 studies on the effects of global warming on plants and animals. He discovered, the risks increase with every degree rise in temperature.

He predicts that if greenhouse gas emissions continue unabated, by 2099, 1 in 6 species could be at risk of extinction. Stuart Pimm, is a biologist and extinction expert at Duke University in North Carolina, he has warned that mankind was entering a sixth mass extinction event, and that the current rate of extinction is 1,000 times faster than in the past. It pretty much seems to be mankind's fault!

"We have all heard of the FTSE 100 index, but we have missed the ultimate indicator, the falling trend of species and ecosystems in the world." Professor Jonathan Baillie, Zoological Society of London's Director of Conservation.

Mankind is responsible for polluting the air that we breathe, contaminating the food that we eat, the water that we drink, and destroying the earths ability to create oxygen that we need to breathe and also its ability to absorb CO_2; if that is not alarming, I don't know what is. It is not just that we are killing off other animals, we are sowing the seeds of mankind's own destruction if we don't stop harming the environment, and start doing more things to actively help it.

4

**Our diet is one of the biggest environmental
issues in the world, but most people have no idea**

If you have ever watched the film Cowspiracy, you'll discover another massive environmental issue linked to our diets. You can quite quickly start to see that environmental issues are much more important that the political attention they receive. A report from United Nations Environment Programme's (UNEP) international panel of sustainable resource management says that:

"A global shift towards a vegan diet is vital to save the world from hunger, fuel poverty and the worst impacts of climate change". United Nations

The production of meat for us to eat, is responsible for more CO_2 emissions than all more than cars, planes and all other forms of transport put together. Despite this, it was reported by the BBC that: "Parents who restrict their children to a vegan diet, could face a jail term, if a controversial bill is passed by the Italian parliament".

5

A tenth of the world's wildernesses disappeared in just 20 years

According to the World Conservation Society Scientists, a tenth of the world's wildernesses have disappeared in the last 20 years, mostly in South America and Africa, and the biggest culprit is unsustainable development, particularly agriculture. It is having a big impact on biodiversity, and is contributing to the massive mass extinction of life that is going on in the world right now.

Do we want to stand before our grandchildren and say we were the generation who wrecked our planet?

I imagine having to stand in front of my grandchildren (if I am lucky enough to get any), and having them ask me "Grandpa, why didn't you do something? Why did you let this happen to our planet? Why did you wreck our future?". If you had to answer these questions to your grandchildren what might you say, "I didn't know?", "I did know, but I couldn't do anything about it? "I didn't care?". It is awkward isn't it. I feel it would be better to be able to say you did something positive, (providing you actually did of course). We all need foresight rather than hindsight in terms of environmental issues. The need for massive fundamental and radical change, could not be more urgent to humanity and all living things. We are sleepwalking into a disaster, and most environmentalists aren't listened to and taken seriously, and seem to have very little influence.

Individual Issues

We are living is this extraordinary time of human history, where evolution appears to be on steroids, and everything seems to be growing exponentially: progress, the population of the world, and human knowledge. The world is on the edge of crisis, economically, politically, socially and environmentally. It is hardly surprising therefore, that we human beings have the potential to experience a massive range of challenges and issues as a direct consequence of all these things.

The Eight Key Self-Issues:
There are eight key issues relating to ourselves, which are:

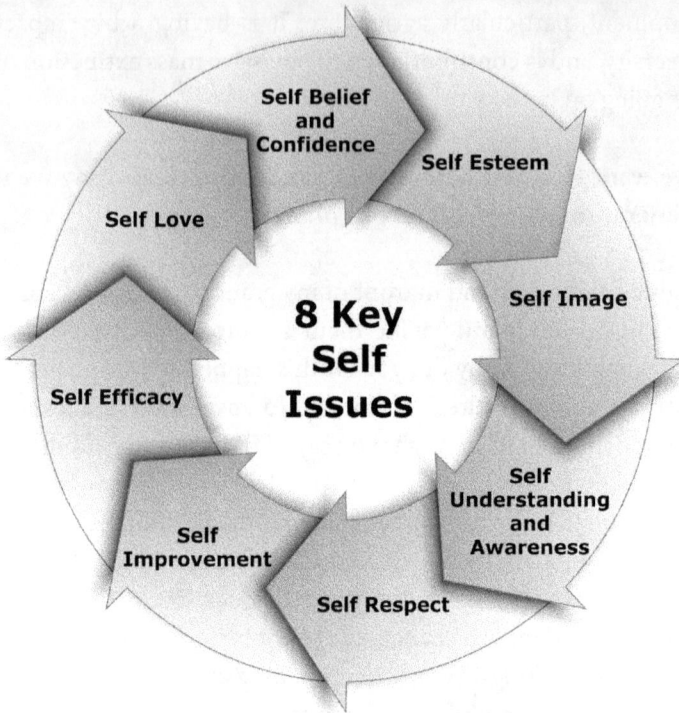

Self Belief and Confidence

Self Esteem

Self Love

8 Key Self Issues

Self Image

Self Efficacy

Self Improvement

Self Understanding and Awareness

Self Respect

1

Self-Belief and Confidence

Self-belief and confidence is all about developing a certainty: about:

- Who you really are.
- What you really want.
- Your values.
- How you are going to achieve your goals and gain the confidence that you will indeed actually achieve them.

If you have self-belief and confidence, you believe: "I can do it. I will do it. I will succeed and achieve my goals".

Believing you can do it, and you are capable of doing it is really important to your wellbeing.

2

Self Esteem

Self-esteem is believing that you are worthy of everything that you want, and everything that you have, and that you are more than fine just as you are.

- Valuing yourself.
- Seeing yourself as important.
- Believing you and your life matters.
- Seeing yourself as equal to all others.

3

Self-Image

Self-image is about how you see yourself; your perception about yourself.

Good self-image is seeing yourself positively. Bad self-image is seeing yourself negatively.

4

Self-Understanding and Awareness

Self-understanding and awareness is knowing who you are, and what makes you who you are.

5

Self Respect

Self-respect is about living your life according to your values, so that you can be proud of who you are.

6
Self Improvement

Self-improvement is about how you grow, develop and improve yourself.

7
Self-Efficacy

Self-efficacy "is the extent or strength of one's belief in one's own ability to complete tasks and reach goals". Wikipedia

8
Self-Love

Self-love is essential for a happy life, yet large numbers of people don't love themselves and the consequences can be devastating.

The big four barriers

There are things that hold us back, stop us in our tracks, block our way forward, make us lesser people, cause us unhappiness and result in us living lesser lives,. These four barriers are: Criticism, Resentment, Guilt and Fear. They can have huge destructive and limiting power on our lives. If they exist they need to be overcome.

1
Fear

Fear is the biggest thing that stops us achieving our hopes and dreams. It not only is responsible for holding up back, it also makes us a lesser person too. Fears need to be overcome as a matter of priority.

2
Guilt

Guilt is destructive, the past is the past; we can't change it. We all make mistakes, so we need to be able to apologise to others if we need to, and forgive ourselves for any of our own wrong doings.

3
Criticism

When you are criticised by others it can hurt, but criticising others is only acceptable if it is done with positive intent, politeness and courtesy, to help the other person to see where they have gone wrong, or how they could improve. It is better to catch others doing things right, rather than doing things wrong. Remember that every time you point your finger to somebody else, there is one finger pointing towards them, and three fingers pointing back to yourself.

4
Resentment

Resentment doesn't serve any purpose other than to make you feel bad and become a lesser person. Let go of all negative thoughts as often as you can.

Problems with our minds

On the one hand, it is possible to say that humanity in the modern western world, has never been better off, we have never had more, known more, been able to do more, but on the other hand all is not well at an individual level. Whilst the miracles of science, engineering and medicine might be able to cure previously incurable diseases and afflictions, many modern lifestyles have caused illnesses, like smoking causing cancer, sugary drinks and calorie laden food causing obesity and an epidemic in diabetes. The interconnectedness of the world means that killer or dangerous diseases like Ebola, Bird Flu, Aids and most recently the Zika virus, have the potential to spread quickly globally. However, the rapidly changing world has resulted in increased complexity, an abundance of choices, which has resulted in increased range of challenges including: pressure, stress, anxiety, depression and an explosion of mental health that seems to just get bigger and bigger. According to a World Health Organisation / World Bank Group Report in 2016, mental health is a massive global issue, with profound implications:

1. "Mental disorders impose an enormous burden on society, accounting for almost one in three years lived with disability globally.

2. In addition to their health impact, mental disorders cause a significant economic burden due to lost economic output and the link between mental disorders and costly, potentially fatal conditions including can- cer, cardiovascular disease, diabetes, HIV, and obesity.

3. 80% of the people likely to experience an episode of a mental disorder in their lifetime come from low- and middle-income countries".

Source: Out of the Shadows – Making Mental Health a Global Development Priority Report

Studies estimate at least 10% of the world's population, of all ages and backgrounds are affected by mental health, and that 20% of children and adolescents suffer from some sort of mental disorder, including anxiety, depression, eating disorders, self-harm and increasingly suicide. In India suicide has now overtake childbirth at the leading cause of death among women aged 15 to 49.4. According to the World Health Organisation, 800,000 people die each year from suicide, and countless more attempt suicide; it is the third leading cause of death for 15-44 years, and in the UK, suicide is the biggest cause of death of men under 50. NHS England reported that 1:4 people suffer from mental health problems each year, 75% are untreated, the NHS spends £9.2bn per year on it. It costs the economy £105bn, and those with severe problems can expect 15 - 20 years shorter

life expectancy. A YouGov Survey in 2016, reported that one in three female undergraduate students said they were suffering from mental health issues, which compared with one fifth of male undergraduates, and a massive 45% of lesbian, gay, bisexual and transgender students. In 2014, there were 130 suicides in England and Wales among full-time students aged 18 or above. 5 Students in York University in the UK committed suicide in just one year. A 2015 survey from the National Union of Students in the UK reported 78%of students reporting mental health issues, with 33% having suicidal thoughts.

Suicide is the biggest cause of death of men aged 20 - 50

If you put all your issues and challenges together, it is no wonder life can be tough

Almost every day there seems to be something new in the newspapers about problems, issues or challenges that different groups of people are facing. As if to help me prove the point, on the day of writing this in the Children's Society's annual report, said that girls in Britain are becoming more miserable.

"Among 10 to 15-year-old girls, the charity's report says 14% are un-happy with their lives as a whole, and 34% with their appearance". Many girls reported feeling ugly or worthless. The figures for England, Wales and Scotland for 2013-14 represented a sharp rise in unhappi-ness when compared with the five previous years. Many celebrities have spoken publicly about mental health issues they have faced, it can affect anyone from any background.

If things are not perfect in your life, you are not alone; if you are feel-ing stressed or anxious or confused about any issue in your career and life, it is very understandable. The world today, is so different to the way the world was, when your parents and grandparents were your age, that it prevents the continuum of wisdom that used to be passed through the generations. Things are changing so fast, that it is difficult for any of us to accurately predict the future, which is one of the things that causes anxiety and disconnection.

In a report by USA TODAY, it was reported that 70% of low-skill po-sitions, 46% of mid-skill jobs and 8 % of high skills jobs, have a high risk of being automated in 10 to 20 years.

Many middle aged people, are finding the world is rapidly changing around them, and the skills and experience they have spent a lifetime acquiring, are often no longer needed or valued. Many toddlers are finding it easier to acquire, new computing and technology skills, than their grandparents or even parents, in some cases there appears to even be an inversion of wisdom, where young people know more about new things that matter, than their elders, who were tradition-ally the custodians of wisdom. Some young people are making vast amounts of money, creating YouTube Channels, providing commen-taries on their boring lives. It is entirely possible for techie young geeks to become millionaires and billionaires in very short time-frames, if they've developed new technology and applications like Google or Facebook that just take off.

Knowledge used to the privilege of the few, now it is available to the many. Knowledge used to be seen as a pathway to better lives and better futures, but whilst knowledge in undoubtedly still incredibly valuable, in a way we have too much of it, we can easily be overwhelmed by it, and not be able to see the wood for the trees. What we desperately need is clarity, simplicity and real wisdom. Much of the knowledge that exists today is wrong or out of date; in the modern world, we need to become as skilled at unlearning things that are wrong and out of date, as we are at learning new things.

It is really not surprising, that it is easy for any of us, to get lost on our life journey and get messed up in our heads, regardless of our backgrounds, and whatever our personal circumstances. It doesn't matter whether you are a prince or a princess, where you are rich and famous, successful or not successful, whether you are old or young, of one religious or ethnic background or another, we are all ultimately human beings, sharing human experiences.

Many of our beliefs, career and life choices and lifestyles, are not conducive to happy, healthy lives and that should be a great cause for concern and good reason to consider change.

I suggest that now is a very good time for new thinking, new ideas and new solutions relating to the way we live our lives and manage our careers.

Take the way you live your life and manage your career to the highest level

You can do anything in life at any level, it is a bit like playing a sport e.g. in football or soccer you have different leagues, from Junior Leagues up to the Premier League in the UK. In other sports, competitions might be local, regional, national and international, right up to world championship and Olympic Levels. When you are playing at the highest level, it is a world apart from playing at the lowest level.

You decide what level to live your life at

Because sport is all about winning, sports people do everything they can to win, taking into account every element that can make a difference. You tend to think that success at playing a sport for example, is all about your skills at playing that sport, but whilst those skills are obviously vital, often the difference between winning and losing, is as a result of other factors which might include: Fitness, Psychology, Diet, Sleep, Happiness, Motivation etc. The highly successful British cycling coach Sir Dave Brailsford was known for the use of the concept of "marginal gains", which was focusing on the tinniest aspects that could make a difference to performance; on their own, these things can seem insignificant, but add lots of apparently insignificant things together, and it can make all the difference.

Most people don't actively manage their life or their career, and I suspect that most feel they don't need to, they might point to their success and contentment with all aspects of their life and career as a reason they don't need to. If on the other hand you have problems, issues or challenges in your life that you want to resolve, you may be much more interested.

Whether you choose to actively manage your life and career is up to you, but if you choose to do it, it is possible to do it at different levels, just like playing a sport at a different level. The higher the level you choose to actively manage your career and your life, the more seriously you take it, the more you put on the table, and the more effort you put into it. It is highly unlikely that you would succeed at the highest levels in sport, if you didn't put in the effort.

Actively managing your life and career is all about impacting the quality of your life. The issue therefore becomes, how important is the quality of your life, and how much effort are you prepared to put into achieving the highest quality of life possible? This book is orientated towards people who want the very best quality of life. I believe that however good the quality of your life experience is, it is always possible to make it better. Circumstances change also, which means that sports people who reach the top of their game, have to work very hard to stay there.

I believe our lives are all so precious, that it makes sense to make the most of our time on earth, what do you think? Do you agree? Are you prepared to put in the effort to do what it takes to achieve that?

I am sorry if you feel I am putting you under pressure, but I am only doing it because I care. I don't think I have ever met anyone who says they are not interested in making the most of their life, but the cognitive dissonance is that most people's actions are not in line with this, yet they find ways to live with this dissonance without being disturbed by it.

The theory of cognitive dissonance was invented by Leon Festinger. The essence of the theory "states that a powerful motive to maintain cognitive consistency can give rise to irrational, and sometimes maladaptive behaviour". Cognitive dissonance theory, explains why people who don't want to die or be ill will smoke, when they know that smoking causes them considerable harm, and could easily result in illness or their death.

The equivalent is saying: I know my life is important, and I really do want to make the most of it, but I am not prepared to do what it takes to achieve it.

My heartfelt desire is to help you to make the most of your life, and to achieve the highest quality of life possible, but I know that there is much more chance that you won't be prepared to do what it takes to achieve it. Someone once said to me: people say you can take a horse to water, but you can't make it drink, but that is not strictly true, you can if you put salt in the horse's oats. I hope that by simply flagging this issue to you, I've put some salt in your oats, and that you will reflect on the issue of doing what it takes to make the most of your life, and achieving the greatest quality of life possible.

In order to take your career and life management to the highest level you need to:

1. *Decide to take your career and life management to the highest level.*
2. *Commit to do whatever it takes to manage your ca- reer and life at the highest level, which includes in- vesting time, money and effort.*
3. *Put everything on the table that can help you to achieve more, be more, have more, do more, know more and make more of a difference.*
4. *Keep an eye on what others are doing and benchmark yourself to do more and better.*
5. *Game Change your approach using the advice in this book.*

Because I know most people won't do what it takes to make the most of their life and maximise the quality of it, it makes those who do very special. It is for this reason, that I've created a community of people who don't just get what it is about, but who actually do something about it. I want to invite you to join me and others in that community if you'd like to.

You'll need to meet the joining criteria. There is a positive energy that comes from joining like-minded people that is uplifting, enabling and inspiring. Living your life at the highest level isn't simply a selfish act, it is about committing to be a force for good in the world as well. For more details go to **www.FeelGoodChangeTheWorld.com.**

Choosing the level you aspire to in life, and operate at, defines you as a person. You can't become an Olympic Champion by being a couch potato. You don't have to be an Olympic Champion, unless you want to be one, but you have to decide how serious you are about making the most of your life.

The best investment you can make is in yourself

We typically spend a fortune on things that aren't important, yet when it comes into investing in how we manage our careers and our lives, we typically invest very little.

If you were to come up with a list of all the things that you invest in, and rank them according to the potential to positively impact your entire life, there is not likely to be anything, that could have to have a bigger and more profound impact, than investing in how you manage them both.

I believe that generally speaking you get out of things what you put into them; a little effort equals little rewards, and a big effort greatly increases the chance of big results.

I remember when smart phones arrived, they were so much more expensive than conventional phones, that it was difficult to imagine that people would invest in them. Many smart phones are significantly more expensive than more powerful laptop computers, with huge screens, yet we have become so addicted to our smart phones, we find them so useful, that we end up paying the high prices. Investment is all about value return.

What value do you put on your quality of life, your happiness, your fulfilment, your career, your wealth and your income?

If you see, think and act differently, you will see opportunities where you previously saw none. People will invest a fortune in gaining new qualifications, with a view to enhancing their career, and it is often a great idea, but sometimes, gaining a deeper understanding of yourself and the world, and gaining access to knowledge, tools and techniques known only by the few, opens up new opportunities, that can create a better improvement in your life and career.

There is another world, known by people who live their life and manage their careers at a higher level, that is frequently unknown to those living their lives at lower levels. That other world, doesn't come with a sign post, it has to be discovered, and part of my life purpose is showing it to others. It is like a secret garden, it is wonderful if you are lucky enough to discover it and can get inside it; there is so much to it, more than this book discusses.

Not investing in more effectively managing your career and life, can result in paying the price of regret, when you get to the end of your life and reflect on the choices you made, and the things that you prioritised. Hindsight is easy, but what you need is foresight; hopefully I've given you some food for thought and motivation to go for it!

CHAPTER 3

THE AUTHOR'S FINAL WAKE UP CALL

"Looking backwards in time with hindsight is useful for learning lessons from the past, but you can't change the past it is history, you can however create a better future, by embracing the immense power of wisdom and having foresight".

Once or twice in my life, a real alarm clock has gone off, I've turned it off, thinking I'll get up in a minute, and then promptly went back to sleep. The most embarrassing moment was when I was invited to Sunday lunch at a distant relatives house. I'd been up late the night before, and I didn't wake up until lunchtime. They had gone to a lot of trouble and had prepared a lovely lunch. They were waiting for me to arrive, and I was fast asleep, it was so embarrassing when the phone rang and I had to explain what had happened. It was particularly hard since it was their call that woke me up, and I didn't even realise to begin with what had happened.

I didn't really wake up properly to how precious my life was the first time, or even the second, or the third time, and now I wonder why? It was a big mistake on my part, and one I hope I can help you to avoid.

I feel it is very easy for us all to go through our life like metaphoric zombies, in a dazed state, not completely conscious of the passing of time through our own life journey, from birth to death.

Often it takes something bad happening to us, or to someone else, that gives us a sense of our own mortality, and in doing so, an opportunity to change and ensure we make the absolute most of our own lives.

It was early evening on February 7th 2014, I was in the dining room at my mum and dad's house, where I was brought up; it was a place where we had shared many happy family meals, but now it was a bedroom for my desperately ill and aging father. I was with my mum, my sister, and my 18-year-old niece Rebecca, who had just started medical school training to become a doctor. We were all surrounding my dad, there was the hum of an air mattress that is given to seriously ill people to stop them getting bed sores, and the sound of an oxygen creating machine in the corner, but worse, was the sound of the death rattle, a gurgling sound sometimes heard in a dying person's throat, until one last breath, and it stopped. Two nurses from the hospice were standing back from the bed to one side behind us, both were crying; my dad was a really nice guy, he had laughed and joked with them in the days and weeks leading up to his death, and they'd become very fond of him. I could hardly believe it; I'd only been talking to him the day before; he was my rock, he was warm and loving and fun and vibrant, and he inspired me, he had been there for me all my life. I loved my dad, and still do, even though he has gone. I really didn't want him to die, but I could only have gratitude for having him as long as I did. I just remember so clearly all the wonderful times we had together, his endless love, his sense of fun, his unfaltering support, and just being there for all the good times and the bad times in my life. In front of me, was the body of my lovely dad, but my dad had gone. It was so startling and final, I'd never be able to talk to him or give him a hug ever again, there was no second chance, no little bit extra. It just struck me, that is was like the early arcade computer games, that used to flash "Game Over" on the screen. If your life is likened to a game, your life starts with you being conceived, and then starts in the outside world being born as a baby, and then one day you take your last breath and its "game over" for your life, at that point there is nothing more you can do or say or experience, in between these two events is your life time. My dad's time was up, he'd made it to eighty, despite having poor health, which was considerably longer than my father in law, Brian, who was sadly taken by prostate cancer at just 57. Each breath that we take is so precious, so life sustaining and also providing us with such possibilities.

When we are young, we think we are going to live forever; the prospect of dying is so frightening for most people, that we can't comprehend not being alive, and therefore try to put it out of our minds. The one thing however that we can be certain of, is that we too will die. Whilst I'd never met my father's dad, my paternal grandfather, I had known my mother's dad, my maternal grandfather, who lived to a good age. When you have seen your grandfather die and then your own father, I very much got the feeling that on the male side of my family, I'm next in line, it will be my turn next. It is like we are on a conveyor belt of time, the longer we are on it, the further we get from

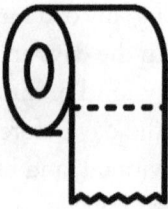

the start and closer we get to falling off the end, and it becoming our "game over".

I think life is a bit like a toilet roll, when it starts off you think there is loads, and it will go on forever, but the more you use, the quicker it starts to go. I think that is why so many of us reach that mid-life crisis point; it's the landmark birthdays, that remind you not just how old you are, but how much less time you have to live.

None of us know for sure how long we have got. We arrive in this world naked with nothing, but a bank account of time. Every day, we go to our bank account of time and make a withdrawal, how we get to spend that time is largely down to us, we can spend it wisely, or we can waste it, the choice is ours. Each day used, represents one day less to live, so we need to make sure that we make each day count.

I've actually had numerous instances where I could have died, and each one has been a wake-up call, but it was a combination of all of them, getting past the mid-point in my life, and seeing my father die, that really fundamentally changed things for me, gave me my true life purpose, and made me take living my life and managing my career to a higher level.

Me having some fun!

1.   When I was about seven, I was walking home from Cubs on a dark night, with torrential rain, this guy

stopped and tried to get me into his car. I managed to run away and even though he got out of his car and came looking for me, I was able to escape, but the police came around and said he fitted the description of someone who had abducted other children.

2.   When I was 16, I spent a summer in Israel. I was walking through a town on my own when this Israeli soldier, moved me and all the other people back from where we were, a small bomb went off which blew a small hole in the pavement and blew out a shop window, I don't think anyone being close to it would have come off too well.

3.   At eighteen, I joined the Royal Navy as an Officer, and four things happened that could have been life threatening. The first happened one night when I was returning to the naval college with a friend. I was doing 70 mph driving down the motorway, behind this enormous lorry. My car was a flimsy Renault 4 with an 850cc engine. With such low power it was touch and go as to whether I would have the power to overtake the lorry. The split second I pulled out to overtake this massive metal pipework fitting fell off the back of the lorry, the sparks were so bright it was like daylight. Had I not pulled out when I did, I hate to think of what might have happened. After that, I set off on HMS Fearless across the North Atlantic Ocean, halfway across we found ourselves in the middle of a hurricane with steady 120 mph winds. The bridge was 80 feet off sea level and at times it felt like we were looking up at the waves. Many of the metal plates of the ship were buckled in, both

the helicopters were written off, and at one time two chefs were knocked unconscious. I was then at the Naval College, and someone ran into our dormitory shouting fire, fire fire, the room was full of smoke, enough that once you were awake, it made you cough. A Libyan who had also been training at the college and who had been kicked out, had set fire to the notice board outside our dormitory, thankfully someone quickly discovered the fire, was able to put it out and wake us up. Then I was appointed to HMS Coventry, I failed an exam, so my joining was delayed. I then passed, was then reappointed to the ship, and she sailed for the Falklands war the day before I was due to join. She was the second ship to be sunk with the loss of 17 lives, and many others were injured. The captain of the ship was the father of famous actress and comedian Miranda Hart.

4.   After the Royal Navy, I went travelling in South East Asia. In Thailand, I had teamed up with an America doctor and we jumped out of a moving vehicle to avoid and ambush, and hid in a plantation in the middle of nowhere, with these menacing looking guys looking for us. On the island of Panay in the Philippines, I came face to face with a group of Guerrillas / Insurgents, who were armed to the teeth with bandoliers of ammunition over their shoulders, looking like they were straight out of a movie set. Fortunately, they seemed like they were going somewhere, so they just walked straight past me.

5.   In 1990, I had perhaps the most dramatic escape of all, I was sailing in the two handed trans-Atlantic yacht race with my best friend Simon, when the

yacht started to break up and leak badly, the floor boards were floating around inside the boat, we headed back towards the nearest land which was Ireland. The steering wheel was smashed off completely. We steered with an emergency tiller until the rudder seized on full lock. We were repeatedly knocked down my mountainous seas with gale force winds. The RAF sent out a Nimrod reconnaissance plane which is massive, like a small airliner, which circled overhead, whilst another RAF team with a Sea King helicopter from RAF Brawdy in South Wales, embarked on a five hour daring and record breaking air sea rescue, that involved them flying to Ireland, refueling twice, with one of those times involving landing on a light house on the tip of Ireland, filling their fuel tank with a barrel and a hand pump, before attempting a record breaking air sea rescue, going further out to sea than any helicopter had previously done. It was all quite dramatic and made the national news. The rescue also involved a massive container ship.

There might seem a lot of these close shaves, but there are actually even more!

There is nothing more important than your whole life, yet we get so caught up in day to day struggles, issues, activities, that we rarely think of our life as whole, and the consequence is that we squander much of our time on earth, without even realising we are doing it.

Don't waste your life, let this book and the words on this page be your "wake up" call. Give priority now to making the most of your life, don't procrastinate, don't put it off, don't be too busy, figure out what is really important and what isn't, and focus your effort and energy on what is important, and not what isn't. Don't waste your life, by living a lesser life, and by not making the most of it today and every day, by not being who you truly are, and being everything that you want to be, and doing things that make you feel most alive.

Authors Story

When I was young, I used to like watching movies, mostly action and adventure ones, I particularly liked James Bond movies. I wasn't a great reader, but there were a few books that really captured my imagination, like Swallows and Amazons, Come Hell and High Water and Come Wind or Weather by Clare Francis, and Reach for the Sky. I remember thinking that I wanted to have an exciting adventurous and rewarding life, I wanted to feel alive, to be energised and excited about life. I used to imagine what it would be like to have the life experiences that I saw in many of these movies, and read about in the books. I developed the idea, that I wanted to become the author of my own life story or life movie.

The result was a life of extreme highs and lows, triumphs followed by set-backs, followed by bounce backs. It's been like a huge apprenticeship, a real roller coaster, with a simply vast number of different experiences, both good and bad, that has given me a unique perspective. It has grounded me in reality, given me humility and eventually turned me into a servant for humanity, with a burning desire to make a difference, and help others on their life journey.

Deciding to become the author of my own life story / life movie

I was brought up in a middle class home. Whilst my loving parents gave me a truly magnificent childhood, I discovered early on, a mismatch between the life that was laid on for me by my parents and teachers, and the life that I wanted to live, so I decided to try and fill the gap through my own endeavours and initiative. I confess, I was a little bit of a maverick, I really wasn't too keen on other people imposing rules on me, if I didn't think they made sense. Fortunately, my parents gave me a reasonably long rein which suited me fine. When I was just 13 years old, I persuaded my parents to let me spend a week walking virtually the width of Wales, which was a hundred plus miles, from near Hay on Wye to near Milford Haven, with my best friend Simon. Sometime during this trip my voice broke, and I came back more of a man.

At the time, I was really interested in two things: sailing and skate-boarding, I embraced both with gusto. I continually found ways of doing things that I wanted to do, which included setting up a business selling watches, getting them on sale or return from the Jewellery Quarter in Birmingham, UK, where I was brought up, and also selling some skateboarding clothing to a local department store. I was the first in my town to get into skateboarding, importing a skateboard from the USA. During my youth, it became a massive craze, and I was ahead of the game. With some friends, I helped form a skateboard club and we ended up, with over 1700 members, we even got the national TV programme Nationwide, and the professional Hobie Skateboard Team to come down to a car park, which we had commandeered as our skateboarding area. I was so excited to meet one of my skateboarding heroes, Mike Weed (www.mikeweedskateboarder.com), who sadly passed away from Leukaemia in 2014. We even got TSB Bank to sponsor us with some T shirts, which all seemed very exciting as a kid.

From an early age, I found my life path and outlook, very different from most of the people around me. As I grew up, I developed a massive curiosity about things I was interested in, I developed a vivid imagination, and a strong desire to pioneer and lead. Many years ago, when I was CEO of a quoted company, one of my non-executive directors, described me as an explorer, adventurer and innovator in life and business. I have slowly come to recognise what he meant by this. An explorer likes making discoveries, an adventurer loves undertakings involving risk and uncertainty in the hope of positive outcomes with the expectation of excitement, and an innovator loves finding new and better ways, and inventing things. That is me to a T.

The truth is that I've had somewhat of a hybrid life, where in some respects I have followed conventional and ordinary career and life paths, and at other times I've experienced much more unusual and extraordinary ones. I believe this combination has given me a unique perspective.

From an early age, I set out to make the most of my life; to become the author of my own life story, to live the sort of life I imagined when watching movies, and reading books in my childhood. The result is a massive series of highs and lows, some really quite extreme, which has translated into condensed learning, that I am now highly motivated to share.

Discovering what the world looks like from different perspectives

I've been employed, self-employed, a business owner / entrepreneur and an investor. From my first part time job as a sales assistant in menswear, with the now defunct retailer, British Home Stores (BHS) whilst still at school, I have done a huge variety of different things in different sectors including: being a Royal Naval Officer, working for 10 years for the Mobil Oil Corporation, which was then the world's fourth largest company in a wide variety of different roles, and having multiple business / entrepreneurial experiences. Along the way, I've become a bestselling author of 13 non-fiction books (including this one) on technology / business / entrepreneurship / sales / careers etc. I've made and lost millions, been pretty much destitute, losing everything during the property crash of 2007 / 2008, and ended up writing 500 + executive level CVs / Resumes, and providing career advice to individuals and on BBC Radio and on a satellite TV Channel that is broadcast to 194 different countries. I've had a mixture of failures and successes, and I believe it has given me a unique perspective. I've discovered that you tend to learn much more when things go wrong, than when they go right.

I joined the Royal Navy as an Officer, but a part of Officer training involves joining a training ship and living and working as a Rating, doing all the horrible jobs including cleaning the toilets. When I was an area manager for a group of petrol stations, as part of my own training I worked shifts as a cashier in a petrol station, and had the nightmare of the console crashing on me on a busy Friday night, not being able to authorise pumps, or take money from people, it was mayhem, tempers were frayed, people were leaving money on the counter and driving off, it was a nightmare. I have long realised that the world looks a very different place, depending upon who you are, and where you are.

How real life can sometimes be stranger than fiction

Sometimes real life can be stranger than fiction, and I think some elements of my life, would be interesting enough to appear in a movie script, like playing cat and mouse with Russian naval vessels during the cold war, being on both sides of search and rescue operations at sea, providing advice to the Iraq Government when Saddam was in power and the United Nations Oil for Food programme was in place, in between the two Gulf Wars.

Whilst at Britannia Royal Naval College in Dartmouth, which is where the Queen met Prince Phillip, I once gave the Prince of Tonga a lift in my car, a battered out old Renault 4, he is now the King of Tonga.

Whilst in Antigua, I unexpectedly found myself in a meeting with the Deputy Prime Minister, who talked of going out for a beer together when he was next in London. In a quite surreal experience, immediately after that meeting, I found myself having afternoon tea with the real James Bond, aka actor Timothy Dalton at the St James's Club. That really felt like being in a movie!

In Kuwait, I've been driven around by a Sheikha, and given audiences with the heads of banks, government institutions, and major organisations.

I've been on countless yachting adventures, including skippering my yacht from Cape Town in South Africa, to the remote Island of St Helena, which was where the British imprisoned Napoleon, some 1,200 miles off the African coast. I have also been on national and international TV and Radio on many occasions, spoken at the House of Commons on childcare related issues, and supported my wife for 25 years who owns a Montessori Nursery and Forest School. Throughout my career, I have so many vastly different experiences, I simply can't list them all, but they include such diverse things as being a British Sea Fisheries Officer, boarding fishing boats in the North Sea and inspecting their nets, catch and papers, working on a Kibbutz in Israel, helping my wife, run her parents Dairy farm for a week, being CEO of a quoted tech company for nearly five years etc., doing consultancy for a company who had invested $3m building a tunnel into an 950 sq km Ice Cap Glacier in Iceland as a tourist attraction. I have also travelled extensively staying in tribal villages, having poor families offer me their only food at one extreme, and then also spent time with multi-millionaires on the other.

Discovering myself

Writing my own CV is a real challenge, there is so much too it. When you do a lot, have a lot of different experiences, meet vast numbers of different people in different situations, experience a huge number of different things good and bad, I believe you acquire a unique wisdom and insight.

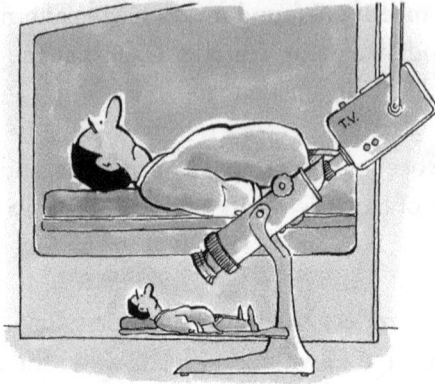

Discovering who you really are deep down is harder than it might seem

I believe that we all see the world and life, through the window of our own experiences. By having so many different career and life experiences internationally, I feel I have had the opportunity to look through many different windows, even though some of them are just for a short time. I also developed a massive curiosity, that made me spend years and years learning researching and studying things, meeting interesting people and interviewing many of them. My experiences and research, has given me a unique perspective, that I hope helps me to serve you in ways that others can't.

I've spent what seems like decades getting to know myself in great detail, and the result is documented in a great big folder 4 inches thick. I now know how to help others to shortcut their own journey of self discovery to a few days. The most valuable thing you can do is learn about yourself.

Hitting rock bottom and discovering my true life purpose

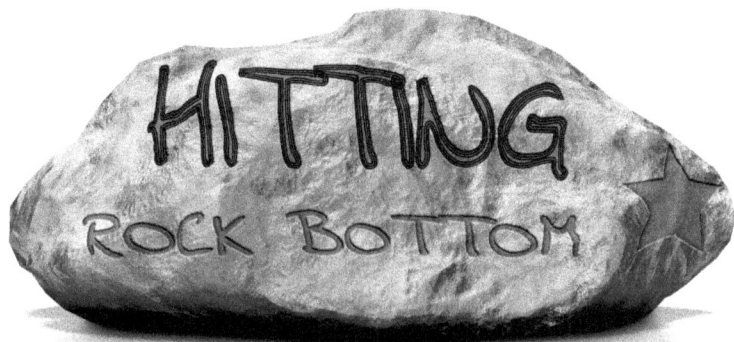

Whilst I have had many highs and lows, it was however during the lowest of low times, during the financial crisis, that something profound happened that changed my entire life, and it was a feeling deep inside, and with crystal clear clarity, that my life purpose was to help others to:

1.   *Live better lives.*
2.   *Have better careers.*
3.   *Run better businesses and organisations.*
4.   *Make the world a better place.*

Call it destiny, call it finding a higher purpose, call it discovering meaning to my life, but I developed this incredibly strong sense that my life purpose was to become the service of others, of humanity as a whole, and of the planet. I started to see, that as human beings, we are all connected, not just to each other, but to the natural world, indeed to the entire universe. We are all part of a greater whole; we should all expect to be happy and fulfilled, and to make a difference.

We all matter equally, we are all different, and I believe there is a place in the world for all of us, we are not meant to compete in hostile ways, we are meant to live in harmony with each other, and the natural world, and we are all meant to care.

As I look back at this extraordinary collection of different career and life experiences, containing huge highs and lows, it feels that it was all for a purpose, like my life had been one giant, and at times, very painful apprenticeship, to help me to serve you and others. It feels like every experience, challenge, meeting or event, was a lesson. Maybe this sounds easy and straight forward, but it was anything but that; for years I had the feeling that something wasn't quite right with my life, that something was missing, that time was slipping through my fingers like grains of sand, that I didn't know what to do, or how to do it. I went from thinking I knew everything, and that everything in my life was sorted, to questioning my core values and beliefs, and my life purpose.

I felt I awakened to a new consciousness and understanding. I really struggled, I went through some very dark times, I searched for help, I read countless books, researched on line, went to seminars, bought information products, interviewing highly successful people whilst making the world's most comprehensive video based education programme on leadership excellence.

Eventually from the darkness in my own life, there was light at the end of the tunnel, which got brighter and brighter. Slowly but surely, I was able to put all the things that I had learnt, and experienced together, joining the dots. The fog of confusion and uncertainty started to lift, and I could see, not just the big picture, but the minutiae too.

A key part of my life purpose is to help others to change the way they see things, think and act, so they can achieve more for themselves, for others, for organisations and for future generations. I help other people to make the most of their lives and their time on earth, by helping them to become authors of their own life story and life movie.

The search for deeper understanding leading to exploration and discovery

Searching for a deeper understanding was hard work

Searching for a deeper understanding was hard work

There is a saying "when the student is ready the teacher will appear", and I discovered rather strangely that is exactly what happened in my life. I have had the gift of discovering and connecting with the most incredible teachers in life, careers and business, that I could ever have hoped for. I've been privileged to have had access to people you couldn't imagine being able to have access to.

The immense curiosity that I have mentioned, was fueled by personal experiences and a desire to achieve more, be more, do more, know more, have more and make a bigger difference, the very same things that I now help others to achieve.

I have the view that if you want to learn anything you want to find the wisest and best people to learn from. When I want to learn something and discover answers, I will be voracious in my quest to find the best answers. It has been a huge investment in time, money and effort, but it gives me the advantage of being able to draw upon it when helping others, to short cut the time that they have to invest to discover the same answers.

I am drawn to the leading edge of things, I like to be ahead of the game, and not behind, I enjoy pioneering, pushing back the boundaries of possibility. I am most comfortable at the vanguard of progress, human endeavour and enterprise. I've discovered, that there is very little in the world that is truly new, even when you think you've come up with something completely new, it is possible to subsequently discover that someone else, somewhere has discovered the same things.

Gaining a new perspective on life

I believe everyone has a life purpose, something that makes them feel most alive, most energised and lit up, in fact so lit up, that their light, indeed your own light, can shine out, and illuminate others and the world, simply by being who you really are deep down.

I think that a good way to think about making the most of your life, is to think about what you would have to be doing, where you would have to be, who you would have to be with, to feel most alive, for most of the time? What floats your boat? What lights you up? What would most excite and energise you?

In a way, I came to learn, that despite the complexity of the modern world, our lives should be simple, all we need to do, is to be who we truly are, and that in being who we really are, we get to do what we are meant to do. We get to play to our strengths, do things that we love and are passionate about, so we get to love what we do. Some people are close to that end point, where their life is perfection, but for most of us, we are some way off that point, many are never aware of it, or settle for lesser lives, or believe that a better life is not possible for them for a myriad of different reasons. I'd like you to believe that you are here for a reason, and that is to take your life and career to a higher level, regardless of your starting point, where you can be:

1.   *Happier.*
2.   *More fulfilled.*
3.   *Make a bigger difference.*
4.   *Achieve the career success you want.*
5.   *Meet your financial needs and desires.*

Life is not about the destination, it is about the journey, reaching new milestones, and moving onto new chapters in your life. You are forever changing, as you grow older, and the world and other people change too, we all live in a dynamic changing world, which is why we all need to be agile and open to change. I want to propose to you that you can be the author of your own life story and life movie too; of course some things happen that are outside your control, but that doesn't mean you should give up on all the things that you can control.

Belief in a need for a new enlightenment

> *"The Enlightenment is the period in the history of western thought and culture, stretching roughly from the mid-decades of the seventeenth century through the eighteenth century, characterized by dramatic revolutions in science, philosophy, society and politics; these revolutions swept away the medieval world-view and ushered in our modern western world". Stanford Encyclopaedia of Philosophy.*

We are now firmly in the modern world, and I believe that advances in science, engineering capability, and an explosion of education and knowledge, have had many positive aspects, but the world is so far removed from being perfect. In fact, we are on the edge of crisis, in almost every way imaginable, and because of that, and the reality of the age in which we live, I believe we need a new enlightenment, that is like a layer on top of the original enlightenment. It comprises three new elements: wisdom, love and imagination. I think our philosophy, society and politics is where our collective challenges lie. We need a profound new view of the world, where we ask ourselves wise and

I've always liked the world "enlightenment", to me it conjures up images of good things.

challenging questions about the status quo, both in our own lives and also the wider world.

Just because we can do things, doesn't mean that we should. When scientists and business owners for example decided that there were benefits to feeding cows who are herbivores food made from other animals, there seemed good reasons, but it resulted in BSE (mad cow disease), which not only resulted in nearly half a million animals needing to be destroyed, but also many human's dying horrific deaths too. Nuclear power seemed like a great idea, until nuclear disasters in Chernobyl in Ukraine and Fukushima in Japan.

Wisdom is all about good judgement and being wise; it is about being able to see the way things are and discerning what to best do about it, and what should be, rather than just what could be. Love isn't about being hugs and kisses in this context, it is about working towards an inspired vision of what can be, doing what is right and contributes towards a greater good. I used to think that being a force for good was an option, now I believe it is an obligation for all of us, it is our duty, and it is the quid-pro-quo of having the opportunity of life on earth. If this feels like a chore, it shouldn't, because the remarkable thing about making a difference, is that it not only helps others, or the planet, it also makes you feel better and happier.

I believe that at this point of human history, we need to take stock of where we are individually and collectively. There are undoubtedly tremendous exciting opportunities and possibilities for the future, but there are also immense problems and challenges, that we need to face up to. Humanity's ability to do extraordinary good things, is matched by an ability to wreak havoc, and do extraordinary bad things to ourselves, to each other, and to the wider world, that supports our very existence, and perhaps even the universe.

I think because of where we are individually and collectively (as the whole of humanity), we need to consider big fundamental changes to the way we approach our careers and life. This book seeks to do this. It is intended to be a simple handbook for life, that helps to provide you will clarity, simplicity, understanding and wisdom, that you can use to help you make the most of your life, and solve any problems, issues or challenges you may be facing.

I'd like to create a positive, peaceful revolution in the way people approach living their lives and managing their careers, so that everyone can be:

1. *Happier.*
2. *More Fulfilled.*
3. *Make a bigger difference.*
4. *Achieve the career success they want.*
5. *Meet all their financial needs and desires.*

At the core of this book is a change of approach that is based upon three elements of change:

1. *Change the way you see things.*
2. *Change the way you think.*
3. *Change what you do and the way you do things.*

Radical change comes from seeing, thinking and acting differently This book is primarily about positively changing the status quo in your life, and implementing change that makes things better and enables you to:

1. *Achieve More*
2. *Be More*
3. *Have More*
4. *Do More*
5. *Know more and*
6. *Make More of a Difference*

"The world has enough for everyone's need, but not enough for everyone's greed." Mahatma Gandhi

Wisdom, Love and Imagination

WISDOM

We are living in the information age; never in the history of humanity, has so much knowledge and information been so easily accessible, and available to so many. Information and knowledge is literally available at the touch of a button, a mouse, or a keypad, and a lot of it is available for free. Super computers have allowed us to process vast amounts of data, which have enabled engineering and scientific breakthroughs. Because we live in the age of computers, almost everything can be tracked, monetarised or analysed.

It used to be in years gone by, that the people who had access to knowledge could have huge advantages, knowledge was power! Now, everyone has access to knowledge, we have so much knowledge, it is easy to reach a point of information overload, where you can't cope with the knowledge you have, let alone take on-board more knowledge.

We need wisdom more than ever before, that can help us to see what is right and what is wrong, what is good, and what is bad, what is possible and what is impossible, so we can make the right choices for ourselves, for others, and for the wider world. There are many people, who I think are wise, like Professor Stephen Hawking and Elon Musk, see technological advances in AI (Artificial Intelligence) as a huge potential threat to humanity, as well as it having the potential to be a very good thing. In a YouGov survey on behalf of the British Science Association, "one in three believe that the rise of artificial intelligence is a threat to humanity".

LOVE

The word love has many meanings, I'd like to be clear I am not referring to anything like free love of the 1960's! In essence it is about being a force for good, caring, being compassionate, kind and empathetic.

IMAGINATION

"Imagination is more important than knowledge. For knowledge is limited to all we now know and understand, while imagination embraces the entire world, and all there ever will be to know and understand." Albert Einstein

Imagination can be incredibly powerful, it is the faculty or action of forming new ideas, or images or concepts of external objects not present to the senses. In essence, it is the ability to think of new ideas, to dream up possibilities, opportunities, solutions, and options of what could be. Imagination is needed to innovate.

When Martin Luther King Jr gave his famous "I have a dream" speech, he was using his imagination, and it helped to change the course of history.

You can use the power of imagination to positively change your life and your career, and to help others to do the same and to improve things, solve problems and create new opportunities.

From Being the Student I Became the Teacher – A Servant for Humanity

CHAPTER 4

YOUR CAREER AND LIFE JOURNEY

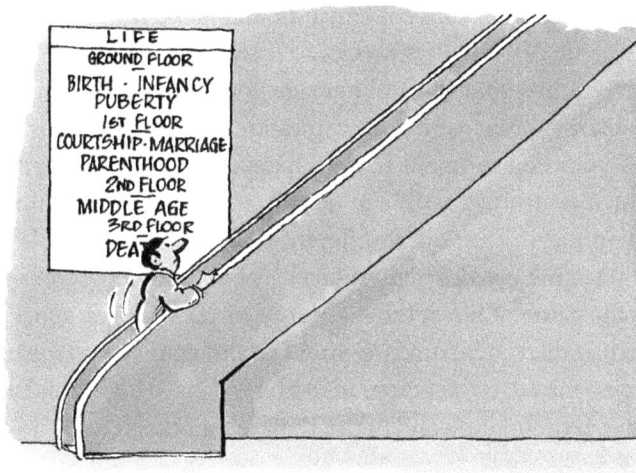

"It is easy to be so busy living your life, that you don't have the time to see where you are and where you are going, and the result is that you can end up living a lesser life, doing things that make you un-happy and unfulfilled and never feeling truly alive and energised. Don't let that be you!"

Are you ready to take the way you live your own life and manage your career to the highest level? I don't want to be pretentious and suggest that I have all the answers, or that I am right about everything; the simple truth is that there are many different ways to live your life and manage your career, ultimately what is right is what works best for you. The solution that I offer you has been created by combining what I have learnt through personal experience, research and study, and also the pioneering game changing innovation I've created. I believe in standing on the shoulders of giants, only reinventing the wheel when it makes sense to do so. I'd like to pay tribute to all those great minds I have drawn upon. You might see some ideas and concepts you are familiar with already, as well as new ones; this book is my take on career and life management. I'll share what I have discovered, what I have learnt, and what I believe. You should be the judge, and draw your own conclusions, and make your own decisions.

Choosing to live your life and manage your career at the highest level is primarily about your own aspiration to make the most of your life, and your commitment to do whatever it takes. It is a subjective decision, it is always possible to do more and better. Just think of the analogy of playing a sport at different levels. Taking your life and career management to the highest level is about making a commitment to play the game of life at the highest level. As with any sport or area of human endeavour, managing your life and your career, the bar is always being raised, so be prepared. Aim high, have high standards and be prepared to do more and better than most others.

Be prepared for an onion

You
And
Your Life

When you take the management of your career and life to the highest level, you metaphorically put everything on the table. Like an onion there are many different layers and aspects to consider, tools and techniques to use. The whole onion looks relatively simple and whole, you don't see the layers until you start to pull them apart, the more layers you pull back the more you see there is to see.

If you were to patiently try to pull all the different layers of an onion apart, you would eventually be left with a pile of pieces. Together these pieces comprise the whole onion.

If you imagine now, that those pieces were actually pieces of a jigsaw you would see that those pieces fit together like a puzzle. Most people will see the picture of the completed jigsaw puzzle, without being aware of how all the pieces fit together, and in some cases not recognising that the individual's pieces exist at all.

When you take your career and life management to the highest level, you open yourself up to seeing that the picture is made up of pieces and learning how the pieces can be used to create an even better picture and end result.

Imagine now becoming the author of your own life story or life movie, where you could create the life and career of your dreams, where the only boundaries are the limits of your own imagination? You get to create your own pictures, you need to make your pictures of your life the most amazing pictures, that would inspire and motivate you, and make you feel happy and fulfilled if you were to be able to make them come true.

Take the red pill like in the film The Matrix

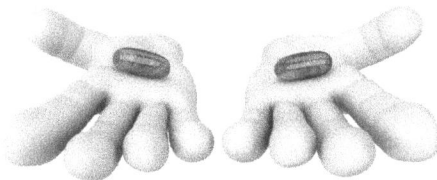

The Blue Pill or Red Pill – What Do You Want to Take?

I don't know whether you have seen the film "The Matrix"? In the film, in a serious moment, one of the characters played by Keanu Reeves, was offered two pills, a red pill and blue pill, and he was given a choice:

"Do you want to know what it is?" said actor, Laurence Fishburne. He then goes on to explain what the Matrix is: "It is the world that has been pulled over your eyes to blind you from the truth." "What truth?" says Keanu Reeves. Laurence Fishburne says: "you can't be told the truth; you have to discover it". If he takes the blue pill, he is told he will go back to his life, and everything will be as it was before, but if he takes the red pill, the truth will be revealed. Keanu Reeves chooses the red pill.

I hope you will find the Career and Life Game Change System™ equivalent of taking the red pill; you'll discover a new truth and reality, that can open up a new world of opportunity, where you can be more in control of the results you desire, and ultimately more successful, happier, more fulfilled, achieve the career success you desire, meet all your financial needs and desires and make a bigger difference too.

To discover it yourself, you need to:

1. Be open minded and receptive to new ideas.
2. See things differently
3. Think differently
4. Act differently

Imagine that you have chosen to take the red pill, and it enables you to see things, and to think things you haven't seen or thought before. Imagine popping the pill into your mouth, taking a cool glass of water and feeling it go down your throat. To begin with nothing happens, then your head starts to spin, your vision goes blurry, and for a moment you disappear into a black tunnel, and no, it is not a psychedelic drug, you are not on some fantasy trip, this is real. You are floating going faster and faster towards a bright light, until suddenly you arrive in this incredible high tech space, a place so advanced, that you instinctively know that nothing like that exists on earth. It has the feel of the Star Ship Enterprise from the film / TV series Star Trek, in fact it could just as easily be a star ship from Star Wars, but it is huge, the scale of the place is breath taking, you feel so small by comparison. In front of you is a big sign "Welcome to Planet Earth Headquarters.

Looking out of the giant window or perhaps it's a screen in front of you, you can see that you are in space looking back towards our beautiful blue planet. It is jaw-dropping, you can hardly believe what you are seeing, yet there is something about the clarity with which you are seeing things, that makes you feel that you are not dreaming, this is real. Instinctively you are not frightened, being there seems somehow normal, you feel you belong, you feel connected, you feel so open that you just know you are ready to receive anything and everything, it is like an instant awakening, a feeling of déjà vu that is somehow normal.

A smart looking guide appears, as if they have been expecting you; in fact, there is a sign welcoming you personally to Planet Earth Headquarters. The guide says "the Chief Executive has been expecting you, please follow me". As you walk behind the smartly dressed guide, your shoes squeak on the highly polished floor. You are staggered by the scale of the headquarters, it is huge, brightly lit, clearly super high tech, and architecturally stunning. The guide is walking toward what looks like a solid wall, you start to look concerned, but at just that moment a door appears, opening automatically right in front of you, and there before you is the Planet Earth Chief Executive. It is the highest tech control room you could ever imagine, crystal clear screens showing every aspect of life on earth, and every aspect of the planet. In comparison, NASA's mission control rooms are nothing.

The Chief Executive says "welcome to Planet Earth Headquarters", we've been expecting you. You sit in the executive chair next to the Chief Executive, the lights in the room are dimmed, but in front of you is a giant high definition displays. The Chief Executive starts to demonstrate the capabilities of the Planet Earth Headquarters, she explains every data source imaginable is available, details of every living thing: plants and animals and organisms, every object natural or otherwise, real time data on all the earth's resources, including sea water and fresh water, energy, minerals and their exact locations and uses. You can be anywhere you want to in high definition instantly, you can see anyone and everyone in real time, and also go backwards to any time in history. You can see clearly all the natural systems in the world working in harmony, you can see all the problems and issues too, and they look alarming.

The information available is like Google, but a billion times better, and every single detail is 100% accurate. It is possible to drill down to atomic particle level, DNA, genetic blueprints, everything you could possibly imagine is all available. Ask any question you can think of, and the answer is immediately available. You can see in real time, exactly how many people are alive in the world, who is dying and who is being born. You just can't stop saying wow, oh my god, I don't believe this, this is incredible, yet because you took the red pill, you know that what you are seeing is the truth, it is real, and you are not dreaming.

The Chief Executive says: "look, I just want to show you something cool", and she says "pick a date". You pick a date, your birth date, and suddenly all the screens are showing the world the second you were born, she selects your record, and there suddenly in front of you is your personal records, every single granule of information and record of your life, she zooms in and you have the surreal experience of seeing yourself born, she hits fast forward and you see yourself growing up, every millisecond of every day is all recorded. She quickly fast forwards to the point where you took the red pill.

You are one of the lucky few she says, you get to discover the truth. On the one hand you are thinking to yourself, this is incredible, but on the other, you are starting to think of all the embarrassing and terrible things you've done in your life, of all the highly personal situations that you rather nobody else could see. Instinctively the Chief Executive voices your concerns, says "don't worry we are all the same boat, and nobody judges you here". What a relief that is.

Rather excitedly the Chief Executive says: "pick any historical event", you say "The French Revolution", suddenly you are there, "pick another she says", "American Independence" and suddenly you are there too, "Signing the Magna Carter", "VE Day in Europe", "Man stepping foot of the Moon", and no, it wasn't a hoax. This is more than just a giant 3D virtual reality experience, there is all the data you could imagine, all the commentary to go with it, and everything is entirely true and factual. You've been gasping with amazement, but suddenly things get every more remarkable, she says "give me a new scenario" thinking on your feet you say, "Napoleon won the battle of Waterloo", suddenly you can see the impact of that. A few more demonstrations and you are beginning to realise the significance of everything, is either positive or negative or neutral. Then things turn closer to home, the Chief Executive shows you all the opportunities you missed and let go in your life, and what would have happened if you hadn't missed or let them go. It was a cold sweat moment, OMG you could be in so much better place in your life and career than you are now. A few screens later, you can see all the key potential turning points in your life, what a relief when you see yourself taking some good ones as well. The data record on you is comprehensive, there is not the tiniest detail missing.

For the very first time in your life, you get to see yourself from the outside in. You can look in a mirror, but it is simply not the same; you suddenly see yourself as others see you, and it is a really pleasant surprise. Compared against every other human being, you are a complete equal as a human being. You are equal to the Queen of Great Britain, the President of the United States of America, to the world's top academics, to the most famous A list celebrities on the planet, to Nobel prize winners, to multiple Olympic champions and to the world's richest and most successful people.

For the first time, you get to see the whole you, and the whole world. You can see that you are made up of four very distinct parts:

1. Your Head
The thinking, rational, logical side of you.

2. Your Heart
The emotional, feeling, intuitive part of you.

3. Your Body
The physical you and finally .

4. Your Soul

This is the I within you, it is the spiritual part of you, it is your identity, it is what makes you, you. It is the part of you that connects you with all other human beings, the part of you that is a part of the human race, the part of you that is connected to the rest of the world and the universe, it is the part of you that just knows, not a knowing that comes from knowledge learnt, but that is instinctive, and all knowing.

You can see that you are a member of so many groups, family groups, social groups, employment and jobs groups, but also a plethora of other groups that are linked to your every aspect of your identity and life. When you work for an organisation, you become a part of that organisation, you are a member of the community where you live, whether you are active or not, you are members of groups related to your gender, to your sexual orientation, to your ethnic group. You are identified by so many different things, who you are is a sum total of all that you are, that you are connected to, and that you impact. You are also connected to the universe, to nature and the natural world.

You've got so many questions you simply don't know where to start:

What is the meaning and purpose of your life? What happens when you die? Is there such a thing as god? Why am I here? Who is really in charge of the World Head Quarters? How does it work? What am I meant to do?

The Chief Executive looks you in the eye, and says: "I know you've got lots of questions, and you want me to give you're the answers, but I can't, because the answers are already inside you, all I can say is that at World Head Quarters, we are not in charge, we can't change the future, we can't tell you what you should do, think or believe; your life is a gift and what you do with it is down to you. We've given you the benefit of clarity of hindsight, but now you need to have foresight" and with that, you were back where you started in the real world.

You need foresight

Maybe that all seems far-fetched to you, but what I hope you can agree is that:

1.　Your life truly is a gift.

2.　You are alive today, and you like most other people, know that you will die one day, but you don't know when.

3.   There are things that are within your control, and things
     not within your control that impact your quality of life.

4.   Even though you might think your life is just about
     you, it isn't, it is about others too, you are a part of
     humanity and the human race, your presence in this
     world has the possibility of creating a positive, negative
     or neutral impact on others and on the wider world.

5.   You can impact not just the quality of your own life,
     but also the quality of other people's lives and of the
     world we live in, by the things that you know, the
     way that you see things and what you see, what you
     think, and the things that you do.

Consciousness and Questions

Consciousness is our awareness or perception of things; you can't
take your career and life management to the highest level if you don't
first develop an awareness and perception of things. It is also more
than that, it is integral to our humanity, to mankind today, and to the
entire future of mankind.

There remains a big mystery around consciousness, where religions
and science collide, where hard facts and evidence are scant. It is important to start to consider questions like:

1.   Who am I?
2.   Why and I here?
3.   What is the meaning and purpose of my life?
4.   What does it mean to be human?
5.   What should I be most concerned about?

I've spent years studying and trying to find the answers to questions like these and more, and I can't say there is a great deal of definitive knowledge. I hope the story of taking the metaphoric red pill will open your eyes to how you see yourself, your life, other people and the wider world. At the time of writing this book it was estimated that the population of the world is 7.4 billion and rising fast. You are not one in a million, you are one out of 7.4 billion, you are part of this incredible tribe of human beings that is humanity.

You need to pinch yourself and remind yourself, that even though modern human beings (Homo Sapiens) are thought to have been around for 50,000 years, you are living in the most extraordinary time in the history of humanity. Bear in mind, that according to Population Reference Bureau estimates, about 107 billion people have ever lived, which means that there is roughly 15 people dead, for every person alive today.

Even though the world itself has been around for around 4.5 billion years, this time in history is like a brave new world; by our collective decisions, the technology we have, and our vast and rapidly increasing numbers, humanity is changing the world at an astonishing rate. We are building town and cities, roads and railways, farming the land, plundering the oceans extracting natural resources, and dominating every living species of animal, plant and organisms, and even pushing out into space beyond the realm of our own planet. We've created a junk yard in space, with all the things we have put into it.

I sometimes wonder if we were to go to the World Planet Headquarters, and see the score card on how we (as humanity as a whole) is doing, just how shocked we would be? Are we doing a good job or a bad job of being custodians of our beautiful world? How do you think humanity as a whole is doing, and perhaps more importantly, how do you think you personally would score? It is an awkward question for all of us isn't it. While you contemplate that thought, I'd like to share with you the story of Edgar Mitchell who was an Apollo 14 astronaut.

Our world is part of a living system

"Whilst Edgar Mitchell was traveling back to Earth, having just walked on the moon, he had an experience for which nothing in his life had prepared him. As he approached the planet we know as home, he was filled with an inner conviction as certain as any mathematical equation he'd ever solved. He knew that the beautiful blue world to which he was returning is part of a living system, harmonious and whole—and that we all participate, as he expressed it later, "in a universe of consciousness."

Trained as an engineer and scientist, Captain Mitchell was most comfortable in the world of rationality and physical precision. Yet the understanding that came to him as he journeyed back from space felt just as trustworthy—it represented another way of knowing.

This experience radically altered his world view: Despite science's superb technological achievements, he realized that we had barely begun to probe the deepest mystery of the universe—the fact of consciousness itself. He became convinced that the uncharted territory of the human mind was the next frontier to explore, and that it contained possibilities we had hardly begun to imagine".

Source: http://www.noetic.org/

David Eagleman is a neuroscientist, who teaches at Stanford University in the department of Psychiatry & Behavioural Sciences. He describes the human brain as "the most complex thing in the universe". I'd like you to pause and think about that for a while. Your brain alongside all other humans, is the most complex thing in the universe, isn't that truly amazing? You and everyone else is very special, in fact we humans collectively are biological marvels.

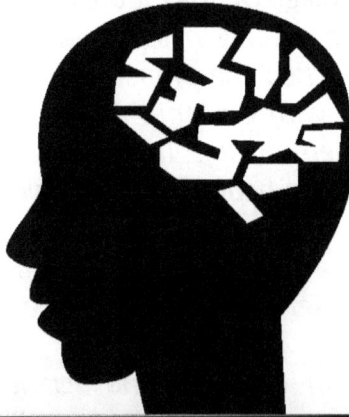

The human brain is the most complex thing in the universe

Whilst humanity has discovered a great many things about the brain, my understanding is that we have barely scratched the surface in terms of what there is to know. His documentaries on the human brain are amongst the most fascinating documentaries I have ever seen. When you start investigating further, you quickly discover that pursuit of knowledge about human consciousness crosses multiple scientific disciplines including neuroscience, psychiatry and behavioural sciences and even quantum physics. Religion and spirituality also consider what it means to be human and what deep secrets lie within our human consciousness. Philosophy also has something to say about it.

1. If humanity is destroying the planet and the natural world, and you are a part of humanity should you be concerned, for yourself, your family and loved ones, for your children if you have any, for other people, for the natural world, for future generations?

2. Is life all about getting all that you can and not caring about others, the planet and future generations?

3. If we are collectively on the wrong paths, economically, politically, socially, environmentally and individually, should we be moving to the right paths?

The chances are that whether you are rich or poor, famous or not, old or young that you've got your own challenges, in that respect we are all the same. Quite often, our personal challenges are so great, and the pressures on us are so immense, that we simply don't have the bandwidth to consider issues other than those in our own lives. If you are struggling to make ends meet, to keep a roof over your head and find food to eat, or simply deal with the immense pressures and stresses of life today, you are not alone.

Earlier on. I asked you to think of a painting of you in your life, you are in the centre, but around you is the entire world, and other people. All the things I have just described are the backdrop and scenery in your life. You are probably already aware of all the challenges that the world is facing, but if you are like most other people, there is a psychological disconnect between these collective challenges and yourself. We often feel instinctively like anything that we personally do, is just like a drop in the ocean, that won't make any difference at all. With that belief, we in effect give up before we even started, we hope

Imagine you in a painting of your life

that someone somewhere, who knows more than us, will know what should best be done and do it. We assume that world leaders, politicians, experts, campaigners, academics will somehow fix the problems. It is like we are on the side lines watching a game being played. We tend not so see ourselves as players in a bigger game than simply our own lives. Without realising it, we tend to do what other people around us typically do. We are heavily influenced by our parents, our childhood and up-bringing, the education system and experiences we had as a child, the society we live in and the status quo where we are that is our normal. Our normal can be very different to other people's normal, you only need to travel around the world to see how different things are in different countries, societies, cultures, environments etc.

> "Be the change you want to see in the world".
> Mahatma Gandhi

When you develop an enhanced consciousness, you start to see things differently and think differently, which is turn can enable you to act differently, which can create the change and transformation you desire to make things better, whether it be your entire life, your career, or the difference you want to make in the world.

I don't know if you have ever bought a new car? There is a strange phenomenon that as soon as you have bought it, you become instinctively aware of other cars the same. The same can be said if you are a lady who has brought a new dress. It can be very disconcerting, it is just that you've developed an enhanced consciousness and awareness towards something.

Consciousness can be shallow or deep. If you pick any area, the majority of humanity will have a shallow consciousness relating to it, and a very few people will have a deep level of consciousness. This is true of the topic of how to make the most of your life.

I hope this book will enable you to achieve a higher level or consciousness. Perhaps you won't be ready to take your understanding to a deeper level now, but I hope if that is the case that you might come back to this book in the future. The deeper your level of consciousness about things, the greater the change and quality of life you are likely to be able to achieve.

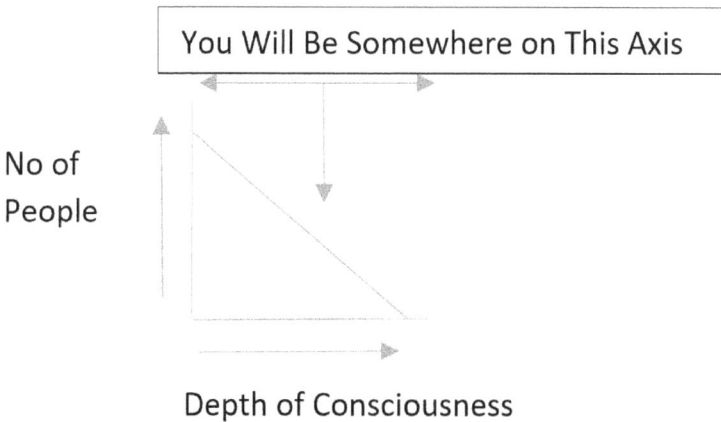

You Will Be Somewhere on This Axis

No of
People

Depth of Consciousness

You can improve your life by increasing your consciousness

I believe consciousness is about more than knowledge. If you think about yourself for a moment, what is it that makes you, you? Is it your physical being? If you were unfortunate enough to be caught up in a terrorist bomb and lose your legs and arms, would you cease to be you? What happens if you were to have a heart and lung transplant or any other transplant, would you still be you if you are living with someone else's organs? Whilst telling the story of the red pill, I suggested that we are all made up of four parts:

Our Heads
1. The thinking logic parts of us.

Our Hearts
2. Our feelings, intuition and the emotional parts of us.

Our Souls
3. The ill-defined parts of us which is the "I within us", the spiritual part of us, that has an instinctive knowing that doesn't come from any gained knowledge, and the part of us that connects us to the universe and the source from which we come.

Our Bodies
4. The physical us.

Neuroscientists have identified different parts of our brains that account for our head and heart functions. Our brains are also known to be the master controller for our physical bodies. Does such a thing as a soul even exist? Is it simply a part of our brain? Is it part of our genetic code, that creates not just the hardware that is our physicality, but also the software that is our head, our heart and our soul? Is it a mysterious energy or force that we simply don't understand? These are all questions, and our consciousness is intrinsically linked to the questions that we ask ourselves. There is so much that mankind doesn't yet know, including mysteries of the universe itself, like how can something come from nothing, is there such a thing as God, if there is, where did God come from, where did we personally come from, why are we here, when our physical bodies die is that the end of us, or there a part of us that continues?

The greater the level of consciousness you develop, you more questions you ask, and the more you search for answers. Doing this, I believe will lead you towards wisdom. Whilst it might seem strange, to gain greater consciousness about things, I believe you need to follow a scientific process, in essence it is about discovering the truth and gaining true knowledge, as distinguished from ignorance or misunderstanding. When you discover the truth about anything, it can change your perspective, change how you see things, how you think and how you act, in other words what you do. The greatest minds and scientists that have ever lived, have asked many of the biggest questions that you will ever ask, and they have all come to a dead end in terms of scientifically validated proof. At this point, all you can do is to use your best judgement to imagine what the truth is. Sometimes when the hard proof is not available, you find lots of signposts pointing in the direction of the truth.

To make matters more confusing, we live in a world where ignorance, misinformation and misunderstandings are common place. Often people in power, control and influence are the greatest perpetrators. They might do this from a position of ill intent, or they might do it, because of ignorance or because they are misguided.

Your consciousness about things can be increased by:

1.   *Personal experience.*
2.   *Developing curiosity.*
3.   *Research and study.*
4.   *Meeting, mixing with and learning from enlightened and wise people.*
5.   *Thinking.*
6.   *Focusing on what you are trying to increase your consciousness on.*
7.   *Experimentation.*
8.   *Trusting your inner feelings.*
9.   *Going into the wilderness and detaching from the high tech world for a while.*
10. *Creating hypotheses and working through different arguments.*
11. *Discussion and debate with others.*
12. *Meditation.*

You need to form your own opinions about how to live your life and manage your career, and how to understand how you relate to other people, the whole world and the universe. I'll give you some ideas, but ultimately you need to decide what is right, and in particular, what is right for you.

Thoughts on us as individuals, other people, the world and the universe

I think it helps to think of ourselves and everything else holistically, in other words to think about the whole rather than the parts. It is only by doing this that we get context, and that we see the complete picture. When you see the bigger picture, you stand the greatest chance of making the best decisions.

All these parts of us, have the potential to positively or negatively impact us, and we can have problems, issues or challenges with all of them. We have the potential to have problems with our career, our life and all aspects of our wellbeing.

Don't get an inflated ego

As we function in the real world, our ego is usually predominant, it is the part of us that makes us feel: 1. We are what other people think of us – that our reputation defines us, 2. That we are what we have – that our possessions define us, 3. That we are what we do – our profession and status defines us 4. That we are what we look like – our appearance defines us etc. Many young people are obsessed with their appearance and how many friends and likes they have on social media. The truth is that only in shallow terms, are we any of these things.

You have to think about newborn babies, they don't arrive in the world thinking, I wonder what other people think of me, or look at me, I'm in a Rolls Royce of prams, or I'm wearing designer baby grows, or I don't like my nose; they are perfectly happy being who they are, they are pleased just to have a body. If you think about it, we were all babies once, we weren't burdened with negative ego or other beliefs, in fact additionally, we were all completely trusting that all our needs were going to be met.

I'd like you to consider the philosophy that all babies are born wonderful and perfect, even babies born with disabilities, simply by being born you are magnificent, a fully-fledged member of the human race, completely equal to all other human beings, even if it doesn't feel like that right now. We are all biological marvels, simply by our creation. The essence of who we truly are, is I believe, our soul energy, and it

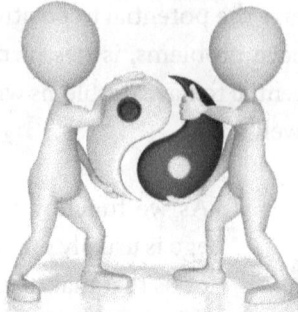

Philosophy is important to the way you live your life

shows up in our lives, in our knowing and intuition, and in the deepest of our feelings and emotions.

I think music, dance and art at its best, when it is total perfection, is coming from a soul / spirit energy, which is why it has the power to move us in the way it does. When we are truly serving others in a selfless way, with good intent, like I believe Nelson Mandela and Mahatma Gandhi were trying to do, I think it is also coming from soul energy. When sportsmen are performing at their peak, or scientists are tuned into their soul energy, magic happens. It is not limited to successful and well known people, it is available to all of us, we just have to find ways of tuning into it. I believe we can all access our soul energy by matching up to it. I've studied what others have said about this, and I believe when we are matched up to the following, we are accessing soul energy:

1. *Love*
2. *Kindness*
3. *Harmony and caring for the natural world*
4. *Beauty*
5. *Creativity*
6. *True pure expression from your heart*
7. *Authenticity being who you really are in the real world*
8. *Being a force for good in the world*

Earlier in my life, I don't think I would have ever thought these things, I would have been a sceptic; but now I feel there is so much more to life and living, than appears at the surface. If we delve deeper and connect to our souls and the universal source from which we came, problems can melt away and we can manifest the life of our dreams. You don't have to be aware of it to access it, but if you are aware of it, I believe you are going to be able to access it for more of the time, until you live your life around it. True happiness and fulfilment comes from soul energy not from your ego, that is why money and wealth on its own, will never make you happy.

If you are an image on a canvass of a painting, why wouldn't you want to see the background and the rest of the picture?

I believe that:

1. *We are the sum of all our parts.*
2. *We are a part of the whole of humanity and the human race, and as such we are all connected.*
3. *We are also part of the natural world, the whole world.*
4. *We are also a tiny part of the universe as well – we are made up of energy and matter which are in effect different sides of the same coin. Perhaps you remember Einstein's Theory of Relativity from your school days? $E=MC^2$.*

I feel many of the problems we face individually and collectively come from the fact that we don't see the whole, we don't think holistically, and as a result, the actions that we take aren't orientated towards harmony between the parts.

I love watching natural history documentaries on television. I have always been fascinated to see documentaries about remote tribes, living in small communities in remote areas. Their societies seem to work really well, they seem to have no problems bringing up their children, they work well as a team, they have hierarchies in their societies which seem to work. The parents teach their children, who in turn teach their children, all that is important. They seem in tune with the natural world, and they always seem to be happy. At times their life seems to be tough, but it is infinitely simpler than life in the modern western world. Reading about early explorers and colonization, I get the distinct feeling that those from the western world doing the exploring and colonization, saw themselves as civilised. I think that even today, many of those in the modern westernised world feel they live in a more civilised world, than someone living off the land and the natural world in a remote tribal village, but given the economic, political, social, environmental and individual problems being faced in the modern world, I am not so sure we compare favourably.

I believe one of the reasons there is a rise in mental health, pressure, stress, anxiety and underlying unhappiness and discontent, is that the choices and the complexity we face in our lives is intense, and the status quo in the modern world, despite social media and technology, divides us up, separates us from each other, and the natural world. If our actions and thoughts are not harmonious, with the whole that we are, and all the things we are connected to and a part of, then I feel we are actually hurting ourselves. There is a lot of pain in the world now.

Earlier I discussed how we are living in extraordinary times due to three factors: 1. The explosion in the world's population, 2. The exponential rate of progress, and 3. The rapid doubling of knowledge. The continuum of wisdom that used to be passed on by parents to their children has been seriously disrupted, because the past in so many ways, is very different to the present, and the future holds immense uncertainty.

As I've been writing these words, our new kitten has been running around, at times trying to climb all over me, I can see it practicing all its cat behaviours. It doesn't go to school, it doesn't even have any parents around, it just comes preprogramed, like pretty much every other animal. Of course some animals learn off their parents, but there are instinctive behaviours built into all animals. A lion or tiger in a safari park or zoo, would most likely attack and eat its human keepers, as they occasionally do when something goes wrong, despite being given all its food every day. The same would be true if you got yourself a pet shark, that had no contact at all with other sharks.

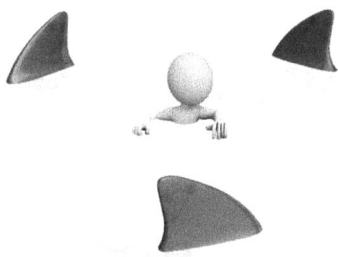

Don't expect a great white shark brought up in captivity not to try and eat you

Put it in your swimming pool and try and go swimming with it, it is likely to try and eat you. Bees don't have to be taught to go and pollinate plants and feed off nectar, they just do it, just like a cow or a horse knows it is meant to eat grass and not other animals.

When astronaut Edgar Mitchell said that he: "knew that the beautiful blue world to which he was returning is part of a living system, harmonious and whole", I think I know exactly what he means; we human beings, and all living things, and the planet and everything in it, are all connected. The late Dr Wayne Dyer, was an internationally acclaimed author and speaker in the field of self-development. He wrote a book that I particularly liked called "The Power of Intention". In his book he refers to others, from whom he has learnt, about seeking the universal truths, that so many of us seek. My own ideas are an amalgamation of all that I have learnt from others, learning from my own experiences and my imagination.

Wayne Dyer talks about this issue of animals being connected to the universe, through which he calls their source, and the concept that universal forces intended us all and everything here, and that it is: "a field, invisible and formless that manages it all", animals, vegetables, plants, minerals, everything is connected to its source. He calls this field or force "intention", and says "the universe is manifested in zillions of ways in the physical world, and every part of you, including your soul, your thoughts, your emotions and of course the physical body that you occupy". If you think about it, remote tribes all over the world, who have no connection with each other, and never have done, yet operate in very similar ways, it seems to me that they are connected to their source. We are social beings, we need each other, we form communities, we communicate, we care for our young and old etc. Remote tribes seem particularly good at living in balance and harmony with the natural world. It appears that the "source" and "intention" that he talks about, is as real for us human beings, as it is for all other things.

Wayne Dyer talks about being a sorcerer, by connecting with your source, which means "attaining a level of awareness where previously inconceivable things are available". I believe in the modern western world, we have huge scientific knowledge and capabilities for all sorts of amazing things, yet in our high tech, super connected world, we have become detached from the natural world, and from our source, and the universal forces of intention that is available to every other living thing.

I believe that the typical modus-operandi in the modern world, is based upon the objective of personally surviving and then thriving. Surviving is meeting our basic needs, whilst thriving is all about achieving success, and success is primarily seen as getting a good job and progressing, or having a good business and profitably growing it, making good money and becoming wealthy, which all enables you to have nice possessions and lifestyle. In many ways, being rich and famous is the epitome of success. Our education system is predicated on the belief that the ultimate success is getting good grades at school, getting into top universities, and into top jobs, that enables you to climb the highest on the career ladder. People who do this are often seen as the most successful.

Often people dedicate themselves to their careers and to the attainment of success as the primary goal in life, regardless of the cost, to their overall wellbeing, their family and relationships and often to their health, and with little or no consideration of their own personal impact to others, to the whole of humanity and to the entire world.

I learnt some lessons about sharing from an Easter egg hunt

When I was a very young child, my parents had some German friends, and we'd go to stay with them, and experience German customs and the German way of life. I remember being there at Easter time, and being desperately excited about the prospect of an Easter Egg hunt, which was something I had never before experienced. The idea was that we would go down to the local woods, where the Easter Bunny had hidden lots of Easter Eggs, the promise was that if we found them, then they would be ours.

I used to love chocolate, particularly Easter Eggs, and I couldn't wait for this amazing adventure to begin. I think I must have been like Usain Bolt waiting for the gun to go off at the start of the Olympic 100 metre final. Finally, we were released, and I was off like a shot, determined to find as many Easter Eggs as I possibly could; this really did seem to me like it was a competition, "finders-keepers". My sister and my parent's German friend's daughter didn't stand I chance, I was off at lightning speed, and before too long, I'd amassed a huge number of Easter Eggs. I couldn't have been happier, but unfortunately rather than just finding the Easter Eggs intended for me, I think I'd found not only my sisters, and our friend's daughters, but I seem to think even some from strangers too. They were obviously none too happy, I had all the eggs and they had none. To being with, I didn't think there was anything wrong with this, after all it was a competition and I'd won, and I wanted my prize. Of course it was never really intended to be a competition, and I was rather reluctantly made to give up all the Easter Eggs that were intended for the others. Even though I really wanted all those Easter Eggs, and felt I deserved them, I recall having a not good feeling inside about it. To begin with, in our early life, we are taught by our parents and teachers that it is good to share, and when others share things with us we are pleased. As we grow older, we realise that true happiness can only come from sharing. In modern society however, we place a high priority on acquiring income and wealth, without realising that income and wealth with no one to share it with will make you unhappy.

Michael S Forbes was a billionaire who liked possessions. He was famously quotes as saying: "He who dies with the most toys wins." Apparently he had lots of boats, planes and toys, everything that money could buy. He had it all: prosperity, power and privilege.

We arrive in this world naked with nothing, and when we die and leave this world, can't take any material things with us. Do we really want to arrive on our death bed and be proud of all the material possessions we have accumulated? Was the collection of materials things what life was really about, or was it contribution, family, relationships, love, experiences, positive emotions and feelings, knowing that we did everything that we could, to leave the world in a good condition for the future of humanity and all the living things in the world? What is the worthiest legacy we can leave behind?

Yvon Chouinard rock climber, environmentalist, and outdoor industry businessman

Personally I am more inspired by Yvon Chouinard, founder of clothing company Patagonia, and his lifelong friend, the late Douglas Tompkins, founder of North Face and co-founder of the Esprit clothing company. Both were adventurers in life, who lived life to the full, who also made millions, after which Douglas turned his attention to pioneering conservation, buying and preserving 2.2 million acres of mountains, rivers, and rain forest in Argentina and Chile. That area is apparently equivalent to about three Yosemite National Parks. Yvon Chouinard is himself committed to environmental activism, and donates 10% of sales or profits, whichever is greater, to environmental causes. When he discovered that cotton was the worst product for the environment, he committed to only using organic cotton in his company's products, to minimise the impact on the environment.

I think "he who dies having committed wholeheartedly to making the biggest difference wins". Life is not really a competition with others, everyone can be a winner in making a difference, you don't have to compare yourself with anyone

Yvon Chouinard provided a good example where the Blain Change Framework could have been used. Until an environmental survey revealed the truth, Chouinard had no idea that large quantities of synthetic chemicals are used in non-organic cotton growing. Cotton growing uses 2.5% of the world's cultivated land, yet uses 16% of insecticides, which is more than any other single crop. What is worse is that the insecticides frequently used are amongst the most dangerous. According to the World Health Organisation, three of the most acutely hazardous insecticides are in the top ten used in cotton growing.

Toxic Fertilisers Used in Growing Cotton Can Seriously Harm The Planet and Living Things

The most dangerous of which Aldicarb, is so toxic that just one drop absorbed through the skin can kill a man. According to the Pesticides Properties Database at the University of Hertfordshire: "It is highly toxic to birds and honeybees, and moderately toxic to most aquatic organisms and earthworms. It takes just under one pound of raw cotton to make just one t-shirt, and to grow the cotton to make that T Shirt, it takes about a third of a pound of nitrogen-based synthetic fertilizer. The fertiliser runs off the land into freshwater watercourses and into groundwater, and some of it makes it way to the sea, creating oxygen dead zones, that prevents all life. Fertilisers are major causes of greenhouse gas emissions responsible for climate change. Who would have thought that the production of our clothes, could cause such massive damage to the environment? As consumers, we are inadvertently responsible for destroying our planet, and most of the time, we are not even aware of it.

Fertilisers enable industrial scale farming, but there is a cost. Bee populations are also on the edge of crisis, populations are falling dramatically and bees are responsible for pollinating plants; with no bees, there is no pollination and no plants. I've had the honour of getting to know Vazhakodan Govindan, who has dedicated the latter part of his life to try to fight the alarming decrease in Bee populations around the world. You can read about his work on the website: globalbeevillage.com.

What alarms me, is the number of hugely important things, that we ordinary people have little or no knowledge about, that can not only negatively impact our own lives, but also those of our children, their children and future generations.

Destiny Versus Free Will Conundrum

There is a very simple question, we all need to ask ourselves, and

that is, do we believe we can influence the outcomes, and the things that we achieve and receive in our lives, by the way we see things, the things we think, and the things we do?

If you don't believe you can influence the outcomes and the things that you achieve and receive in your life, you leave everything to chance, and all you do is hope you end up somewhere you want to be. You become like a piece of flotsam, floating on the ocean of life; you have no idea where you will end up, and you have no control. Where you end up, is simply down to destiny, fate or the will of others.

If, however, you believe you can have control over the outcomes and things that you achieve and receive in life, why haven't you used that control to get the life and career that you want? Perhaps you have, but most people won't, and there are four probable reasons, and even if you have, a totally awesome, incredible life and career, it is always possible for them to be even better:

1. *You simply haven't taken control of your life?*
2. *You don't know how to take control of your life?*
3. *You have tried to take control but external factors have kyboshed your efforts?*
4. *The control that you have taken hasn't been that effective?*

It is not what happens to you in life that really defines you, it is what you proactively bring into to your life, and how you respond to events and situations outside your control. Do you become a victim, feel sorry for yourself or give up, if factors beyond your control, give you less than you want, or do you use the experience, setback or challenge, to learn, to grow and to improve, to make you stronger and wiser? When opportunities come your way do you see them and seize them or remain blind to them and ignore them?

If you choose to become the writer and director of your own life movie and the author of your own life, you need to understand, that you don't live your life in isolation, your life will be influenced by external events, and others, and factors not within your control.

I'm a keen sailor, and I know that you can't change the wind, but you can change the cut of your sails or the destination you head towards. It is impossible to sail directly into the wind, your sails flap about wildly, they can make a terrible noise, and you tend to drift backwards. If you want to sail towards the wind, you need to tack, in effect taking a zig zag course, pointing no closer than about 45 degrees to the wind. Sometimes in life, you will find you can't get what you want immediately, you need to be patient, and to work towards a goal, getting there, step by step, perhaps having to zig zag rather than aiming straight for your desired destination. A wise sailor always keeps their options open, and changes course when necessary, you need to do the same.

You can't write your life story in stone, you need to remain flexible and resilient, and alter course and change your goals if you want to or have to, taking into account changed circumstances; the truth is, that what you want, will change over time. Being the writer and director of your life movie, and author of your own life story, isn't a one off exercise, it is something you need to continually work on, responding, not just to big fundamental things, but also small things on a daily basis.

It is easy to get confused and to either believe either destiny and external forces are in charge of your life, or that you are completely in control. Many people are not sure which is true. I often hear people of faith describing events in their life as "God's will". Some people who are into astrology, will get a reading that tells them what is going to happen in their life, as if it is already pre-determined.

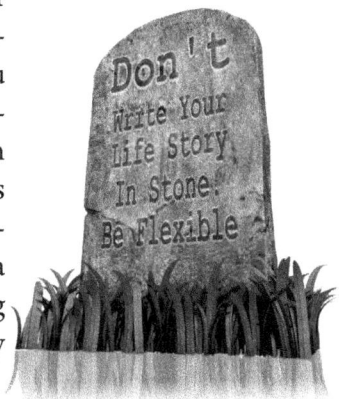

The two choices would appear to be:

1.   *Destiny.*
2.   *Free Will or Intention.*

The concept of destiny, is that an external power / forces perhaps even God, is believed to control what happens in your future life or maybe it is just random events, over which you have no control, whereas the concept of free will and intention, is that you shape your own life, by setting out to achieve a goal, and purposefully and progressively work towards the achievement of that goal, doing practical tasks until you achieve it. I believe that the truth is that both these things are true.

Most people will set out to achieve some things using their free will and their own intention, but will also be happy to pursue a path or course of action in life, and see where it takes them, leaving it up to destiny. It is a choice between defining the goal or defining the direction and not have a specific goal. All of us are subject to external forces, which could be other people directly, or the political, social, economic or environmental circumstances / factors. We don't know if we will be struck by lightning, run down by a drunk driver, blown up by a terrorist, or win the lottery, have someone show us a random act of kindness, or have some other good fortune bestowed upon us. Sometimes all it takes is to be in the right place at the right time for something good to happen, or to be in the wrong place, at the wrong time, for something bad to happen.

Universal forces that can enhance your life

There is a third concept, that I describe as: "Universal Forces". Not everyone will agree that they even exist. If destiny is where external forces make things happen and shape your life, without you having any input whatsoever, and intention is where you decide you are going to do something, you create a strategy of how to achieve it, you translate a strategy into a plan that you can implement, you then take action. Universal Forces are like a bolt on success turbo, onto free will and intention; where you are able to call upon forces consciously or subconsciously, to deliver outcomes that you want.

In the 1800's the concept of the "Law of Attraction", first arose, which is central to books like Napoleon Hill's Think and Grow Rich, You Can Heal Your Life, by Louise Hay, and more recently the multi-million best-selling book / film The Secret, the basis of it is that:

"Like attracts like" which in New Thought philosophy, is used to sum up the idea, that by focusing on positive or negative thoughts, a person brings positive or negative experiences into their life. This belief is based upon the idea that people and their thoughts are both made from "pure energy", and the belief that like energy attracts like energy.
Wikipedia

These universal forces are both within you and within others, and include things like:

1.	Inspiration (which comes from being "in spirit")	9.	Commitment
2.	Passion	10.	Courage
3.	Energy	11.	Mindset / Attitude
4.	Enthusiasm	12.	Desire
5.	Belief	13.	Positivity
6.	Imagination	14.	Presence
7.	Motivation	15.	Emotion
8.	Resolve / determination	16.	Charisma

You see some people who light up the world by their presence, their passion, energy, enthusiasm seem to radiate from them, they touch hearts and souls, they evoke emotions, and what they've got spreads to others. Have you noticed how sometimes life, just radiates out of people, they move us in every respect. Some sports people seem unstoppable; you just know they will prevail. In extreme circumstances, people have been known to gain superhuman strength, to lift a crashed car off and injured pedestrian, or on the battlefield, some people will defy the odds, and commit acts of extraordinary bravery, risking their own lives to save the lives of others.

There are many who believe in the intangible force called spirit, which is said to be "capable of healing, creating miracles, manifesting and making a connection to divine intelligence and genuine possibilities" Dr Wayne Dyer. referred to "source", meaning the intangible force from which all things, living and other come from, a force that intends the being of everything. It was defined by Patanjali over twenty centuries ago as "dormant forces, faculties and talents come alive, and you discover yourself to be a greater person by far, than you dreamed yourself to be." Carlos Casteneda, referred to sorcerers (those who live in the source), to call upon these intangible forces to set up a path for attainment of something.

It is nice to think of there being incredible forces in the universe that you can access, to help you achieve and manifest anything that you want. There is advice available about how to connect with this force. Whether you believe this or not is for you to decide.

Overcoming setbacks and challenges

We Are All Tested

In 1995, I met an 18-year-old girl, who had a dream to go racing yachts. She didn't really have much experience racing yachts, and she had very little money, in fact, she lived on less than 50 pence (75 US Cents) a day for food, which she either ate cold, or cooked in an electric kettle. She lived in a tiny 8ft by 10ft portable building in a boat yard, which contained a desk and a chair, and had a mattress on the floor. She rode everywhere on her bicycle, because she couldn't afford public transport, let alone a car. She was desperate to gain sponsorship, she worked hard on people's boats to earn some money, to buy some stamps, some paper and printer toner. She sent off thousands of letters, but no one was interested, most people didn't even bother to reply. It was a great disappointment, but she didn't give up. Ten years later the BBC paid for me to go to Falmouth on the South Coast of the UK, put me up in a hotel overnight, and interviewed me on an incredible £multi-million racing trimaran. This young girl was now 28, her name was Ellen Macarthur, and she had just become the fastest person to sail around the world, having sailed 26,000 miles in 71 days, 14 hours, 18 minutes and 33 seconds. She was made the UK's youngest Dame. There were tens of thousands of people there to greet her back to the UK, and the media was there from all over the world.

It was a far cry from those days in the boat yard, where nobody was interested. She is now marketed by a speaker's bureau to deliver keynote talks for between £10K - £25K. Having achieved extraordinary things in sailing she dedicated her life to a charity supporting children with cancer, and in encouraging organisations to be sustainable.

We choose our own levels, even if we don't consciously think about it. Like a sportsman you can make a conscious decision to play your game at any level, from a novice up to world champion / Olympic gold medal level.

There comes a time, particularly if we've achieved setbacks, challenges or issues, that rather than fight and strive, to reach the level we truly deserve, we give up, we stop believing, perhaps we never believed at all, and the mould becomes set. It could be that we've embraced excuses: we are not smart enough, we don't have the right qualifications, we don't have the right connections, we are too old, too young, we went to the wrong school, we made the wrong decisions, it is too late for me to do anything now. These excuses are like a shield protecting us from the ultimate truth, that there is nearly always a way, if there is a will. It is easier to blame external circumstances, or other people, than it is to blame ourselves for giving
up, lowering our standards, or not being prepared to do what it takes, to positively change our status quo. I know from bitter personal experiences, that at times, life can be tough; your best efforts can fail, and the light can seem to go out at the end of the tunnel, but remember light will always follow darkness. Don't give up too soon, or settle for less than you truly deserve.

You might not have any problems you can quantify, you might just have that vague feeling that something isn't quite right, that you are not as happy or as fulfilled as you think you should be.

Perhaps you are already riding the crest of a wave, your life and career are great, but you just want to achieve even more, the solution for doing this, or solving problems is the same.

If you don't have the resources you think you need, then you need to get resourceful. If you don't have the contacts you think you need, you need to make them. You have to use what you have, make the most of what is available to you, if this way doesn't work, try another way, if you don't succeed first time, learn from your experiences, improve, change and try new strategies, or simply be persistent and never give up. Work harder and smarter, be different, but better, be your true authentic self. Be creative and adopt innovative new strategies, do things that have never been done before.

Even if you feel you have nothing at all, it is quite possible to make something from nothing, but the reality is, you are: more special, more powerful, more capable, and more awesome, than your probably imagine you are. Just because you might be blinded to the brilliance within you, doesn't mean that it is not there.

Don't accept that the mould is set, that your life can never change for the better, it can and it will if you diligently follow the advice in this book. The only time you are truly beaten is when you give up.

CHAPTER 5

CAREER AND LIFE GAME CHANGE SYSTEM

"It would be nice if our lives could be a steady progression towards incredible things, but they are typically full of challenges, twists and turns, that could easily result in us living a lesser life than we would like, unless we learn how to best navigate the inevitable ups and downs we will experience".

When we are born, we don't arrive with a handbook, a set of instructions about how to live our life, or indeed a set of goals of what we need to achieve.

As a baby we cry when we want food or drink, when we want our nappies changed, or when we want something that we are not getting, or if we don't like something. Our parents or carers make the key decisions for us, which are typically based on what other people do, and what the law says we have to do and can't do. At school our teachers take over from our parents and carers, and we get educated. We observe and experience the world around us, we interact with others and are influenced by a multitude of different things. Eventually we become adults where we become free to make more choices about our lives. There are some restrictions on what we can or can't do, we are governed by laws and what is deemed acceptable by others. In organisations there are rules, policies and procedures that we also have to follow.

We tend to just look to our next immediate goal and not think of our lives as a whole

Generally speaking, we don't think too much about our lives as a whole, we tend to focus our attention on where we are, orientating our effort on what we need to achieve, accomplish or do next. It is like we have a horizon, a distance into the future that we see, which represents our immediate goals.

Whilst there are many different educational and career paths, which may involve vocational qualifications and apprenticeships, a common path in the UK, is doing GCSE exams at age 16, with A-Level exams at age 18, after which many people go to University. Two years before taking your GCSE exams you have to choose which subjects you want to take. My middle daughter did 12 subjects at GCSE, but is doing just four at A Level. The subject choices you take at GCSE, impacts the choices of A Level subjects, which impacts which subject you do at University, which can impact what career you end up doing. Whilst university courses, don't have to be related to the career that you go into, they often are. Whilst there are many different career paths available, and vocational training and apprenticeships as well, the point I am trying to make, is that often decisions taken very early in life have led you to where you are now, and the path you are on, that if you don't change, will take you to a certain place in the future.

When we made subject choices at school, we had very little idea of what career and life possibilities were available to us. It is entirely possible that we didn't make the best choices. Nobody told me what the goals of my life as a whole should be. All we typically know is that when we grow up, we need to earn a living and have a career, which we usually think in the first instance that is likely to be a job working for someone else.

There are four principal ways you can earn a living:

1. *Employed*
2. *Self Employed*
3. *Business Owner*
4. *Investor*

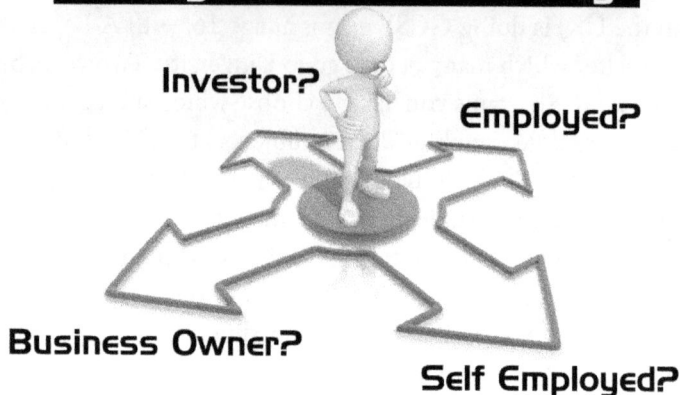

4 Ways To Earn a Living

Investor?

Employed?

Business Owner?

Self Employed?

When you are employed or self-employed, you are typically swapping your time for money and other benefits your employer might also offer. Because your time is finite, your earnings are limited. If you stop working, you stop earning. As a business owner you can earn money in different ways, selling products and services, leveraging the value of labour, intellectual property or assets etc. As an investor you can make money from rental income, dividends, interest and asset appreciation etc. As an investor, your money can do the hard work for you.

I've had experience in all four areas, they each have their pro's and con's, I'm not going to suggest you do one or the other, in fact you can change how you earn a living during the course of your life and it doesn't have to be an either / or decision, you can potentially do them together.

Gary Dutton, whose autobiography I published, left school aged 16 with no qualifications, his teachers said he would never amount to anything, but now he is worth approx. £130m, he has an executive jet, his own little mini cruise ship and a fleet of exotic and luxury cars. At one time he employed 1000 people and was awarded an MBE in the Queen's New Year's Honours for Services to Industry. His story is described in his autobiography which I helped him to write and publish.

We typically think of having a career to "earn a living", which is to earn enough money to pay for everything that we need. To earn a good living means to have enough money to live a comfortable living as opposed to a basic living.

The career and life game change system is a radically new approach to live your life and manage your career, based on seeing things differently, thinking differently and doing different things or things differently.

Career and Life Game Change

Imagine for a moment buying a board game. When I was young I remember liking playing two board games: Monopoly, which was about making money, and Cluedo, which was a murder mystery game, where you had to work out who had committed the murder, in what location, and with what weapon.

Every board game comes with a set of instructions of how to play the game, which specifically defines the objectives of the games and the rules of the game. We've already discussed that when you arrived in the world, you didn't arrive with a set of instructions of how to play your life, with rules you needed to follow and what the objective of your life is. I'd like you to imagine now that your life is a board game, you are one

Imagine your life was a game - you need to become a good player

of the characters in the game, and you are already part way through the game. You didn't think your life was a game, you were just in it, getting on with it, but now you've been made aware you are in it, and you are being offered the opportunity to use your new awareness to "game change" if you think it is appropriate. If you want to, you can fundamentally change the way you play the game, and how you see your life and career, and the choices that are really available to you, with the purpose of making your future better than your past.

See this opportunity as a wake-up call, or simply an opportunity to help you to take stock of where you are now, where you want to be, what you want to do with your life and career.

There was a film called the Trueman Show:

Actor Jim Carrey, plays Truman Burbank, who "is the unsuspecting star of The Truman Show, a reality television program in which his entire life, since the moment of his birth, is filmed by thousands of hidden cameras, 24 hours a day, 7 days a week, and is broadcast live around the world. The show's creator and executive producer Christof is able to capture Truman's real emotion and human behaviour when put in certain situations. Truman's coastal hometown of Seahaven is a giant set built under a giant arcological dome in the Los Angeles area. Truman's family and friends are all played by actors, allowing Christof to control every aspect of Truman's life". Wikipedia

What a shock it would be to all of us, to find out that we were characters in someone else's game or movie?

Our instant reaction is to think, I am not Truman Burbank, that is not happening to me, I am in control of my own life, but are we really as in control as we think we are? Throughout the history of mankind, people of power and influence, have been controlling and influencing, and benefitting from the labour and work of others. Just think about the 1% of the world's population who earn more than the other 99% combined. In the days of slavery, you knew if you were a slave because you had shackles around your legs, and slave masters with whips, keeping you in control. These days we willingly submit to work for others for a salary / wage and benefits. Other people frequently profit from our labour. I am not saying there is anything wrong with that necessarily, but in the modern capitalist, consumer driven society, we have been conditioned and persuaded that we need lots of things, that we spend our hard earned money on, which frequently makes other people rich. If our lifestyle can be improved throughout our lives, we are often happy, with things like: bigger, better, cars, houses, holidays, smart phones and other products and services and we feel satisfied. If our lifestyle reduces through unemployment or other reasons, we tend to be unhappy. We build very strong ideas about what we are worth, what is good and bad for us, but our scale is often very different to the super wealthy. Most of us believe that executive jets and our own mini cruise ships are beyond us, yet when or if you get to that level, you can start to be concerned with the next executive jet and mini cruise ship up the range, everything is relative. The state is also taking their cut in terms of taxation. There is a truth that super rich, highly successful people don't see the world in the same way as ordinary people, they don't think the same way and they don't do the same things. Some might argue that it is a conspiracy of the rich to keep the poor happy with what they've got, but I don't think that is the case.

Most people assume that the goal in life is to be successful, and a common definition of that is wealth and eminence. Do you think that is our collective goal in life? Why is it that so many people who become hugely successful and achieve considerable wealth and fame, are often so unhappy, so much so, that some commit suicide, and many like Bill Gates, Warren Buffet and most recently Mark Zuckerberg, decide to give away most of their wealth?

Money and wealth in itself does not make you happy, but it gives you choices, and it can take away financial pressure and stress. We all dream of winning the lottery, but many people's lives are ruined by winning. You might think I am crazy; I'm not saying don't go for money, all I am saying, is that money shouldn't be the goal in itself, it is what you do with it that really matters.

His Holiness The 14th Dalai Lama

The meaning and purpose of your life

"ONE GREAT QUESTION underlies our experience, whether we think about it consciously or not: What is the purpose of life? I have considered this question and would like to share my thoughts in the hope that they may be of direct, practical benefit to those who read them.

"I believe that the purpose of life is to be happy. From the moment of birth, every human being wants happiness and does not want suffering. Neither social conditioning nor education nor ideology affect this. From the very core of our being, we simply desire contentment. I don't know whether the universe, with its countless galaxies, stars and planets, has a deeper meaning or not, but at the very least, it is clear that we humans who live on this earth face the task of making a happy life for ourselves. Therefore, it is important to discover what will bring about the greatest degree of happiness." Dalai Lama

You are probably reading this now, because you, like just about everyone else, has a massive curiosity about the meaning and purpose of your own life, that surfaces every now and again; typically, because either something happens, like you, or someone you know, suffers a life threatening illness, or accident, or perhaps even losing someone dear to you. It can also be a landmark event, like a birthday or a new year, or a feeling that you have, that your career and your life aren't great. Surprisingly, it often takes something bad happening, or even the contemplation of death itself, to make us really think about our lives.

Our instant reaction, is to think that the meaning and purpose of your own life, is a deep question, so deep in fact, that we possibly can't hope to ever find out. The meaning and purpose of life in general, is something that we think is beyond the ordinary man or woman, it is something that is contemplated by ultra-wise and intelligent people, typically thought to be theologians, philosophers, scientists or academics.

The definition of meaning is: "something meant or intended" and the definition of purpose is: "reason for which something exists or is done". Meaning and purpose are very similar, in simple terms, I believe it is better to think of it as two simple questions:

1.　*Why are you alive?*
2.　*What are you meant to do with your life?*

The first question: "why are you alive" is interesting, and it would be definitely nice to know the answer, but the second question seems a much more pressing one to answer, because you make decisions every single day about that.

I bow my head in respect to the great philosophers, theologians, scientists and academics, who have attempted to answer these questions, but I would like to offer you my own thoughts on this topic, that I hope you may find useful.

I believe that you are alive because forces unknown to us in the universe, intended you to be alive right now; you are not here by accident, or chance, and you are just as important as everyone else who is also alive today. I also believe that your life is a precious gift, and what you need to do, is to really live your life to the full, to make the most of it, by specifically setting out to achieve the following five things, which comprise 3 primary goals and 2 secondary goals:

Primary Goals of Life

1.　*Be Happy.*
2.　*Be Fulfilled.*
3.　*Make a difference in the world.*

Secondary Goals in Life

1.　*Achieve the career success you desire.*
2.　*Meet your financial needs and desires.*

All these five things are related. First however, we need to survive and stay alive; we need food to eat, water to drink, air to breathe, temperature control, perhaps needing either warmth or cooling / shade, and shelter from things that can harm us. In simple terms, I believe our goals are to:

1. *Survive.*
2. *Then thrive, but it is just not thriving, it is achieving complete contentment, happiness and fulfilment.*

I believe that as human beings we are all connected in some way, we are all a part of the human race, and also a part of the universal whole, e.g. a part of everything that exists in the universe. Whilst we share many characteristics, we are all different, no two human beings look exactly the same, even identical twins have some physical differences, but inside we are all wired slightly differently, we have different preferences and tastes, hopes, dreams and aspirations; we are all unique.

Abraham Maslow was a psychologist, who wrote a paper called "A theory of human motivation", which was subsequently was described as "Maslow's hierarchy of human needs", and is represented in the form of a pyramid / triangle shape. The highest level was "self-actualisation", which is the concept that "whatever a man or woman can be, he or she must be", it is really about fulfilling our personal potential. In later life, he changed his views slightly, and added another layer called "Self-Transcendence", where he said: "the self only finds its actualization in giving itself to some higher goal outside oneself, in altruism and spirituality".

To enable you to:

1. *Be Happy.*
2. *Be Fulfilled.*
3. *Make a difference in the world.*
4. *Achieve the career success you desire.*
5. *Meet your financial needs and desires.*

I believe you need to go on an inner journey to discover who you really are deep down, when you know that, all you need to do is to be your true self, to be who you really are deep down, in the real world. Whilst what you do with your life, obviously matters a lot, when you are being who you really are and self-actualising, what you do, becomes a by-product of being who you are. Being who you really are is really important; that is why we are called "human beings" and not "human doings".

The most wonderful thing, is that when you make a shift, to release the "real you" in all your glory, you will discover that you are a far greater person, than you could ever imagine yourself to be. You are capable of achieving more than you could imagine, feeling more alive than you have every felt in your life before, being happier, more fulfilled, and also making a difference in the world.

There is a great quote from Buddha:

"Your work is to find your work, and then give yourself to it with all your heart".

By that, I believe he means your life's work. The best part of working towards this is that you:

1. *Get to be who you really are.*
2. *Get to do what you love, so that you end up loving what you do, that makes you feel fulfilled.*
3. *In doing this, you are playing to your strengths, therefore leveraging maximum value from your uniqueness.*
4. *You get to achieve the career success you desire, whatever that might be, meet your financial needs and desires, be happy and fulfilled and make a difference in the world.*

In Control or Out of Control

LIFE BY CHANCE
"Followers in Life"

"Relatively few decisions, and largely see where life takes you"

LIFE BY DESIGN
"Leaders in Life"

"Know who you are, what you want, have a strategy and plan and every day move closer to your goals".

The biggest choice you'll ever make in your life, to whether to be in control of your life and career, or not in control.

Choose to be in control of your life and become a "leader in life"

Choosing to be in control of your life and career, is about choosing to design your life; of course unforeseen things might happen, that are beyond your control, but if they do, you simply modify your plans, as and when you need to. It doesn't mean having to stick to a path that no longer seems right, in fact it is good if you refine your goals, any time you need to. You have to be agile to respond to opportunities and defend against threats, and also to continually try and connect with your authentic self, and just be the person you really are deep down, and the very best of you.

Most people, by not making a conscious decision to be in control of their life, by default take the other path; it is not to say that there is no decision or choices, of course there will be, but there is no overall clear set of objectives for the short, medium and long term, and no game plan or carefully thought through strategy to be able to achieve it.

When you are in control of your life, you are a leader in life, leading yourself, when you are a follower in life you do very similar things to the majority, make relatively few decisions and largely seeing where life takes you.

Being a leader in life you are being largely active in the way you live your life, and being a follower in life you are largely passive. Leaders in life are predominantly proactive, and followers in life are predominantly reactive.

Leader in Life	Follower in Life
Mostly In Control of Life and Career	**Mostly out of Control of Life and Career**
Knows clearly what they want in the short, medium and long term, documents it, and has a game plan/ strategy of how to achieve it and every day moves towards achieving the goals	Doesn't know that clearly what they want, doesn't document it, thinks predominantly short term, gets on a path and sees where it takes them without thinking too much about the big picture.
Forever Adjusting Your Course	Rarely Adjusting Your Course
Mostly Active at Managing Career	Mostly Passive at Managing Career
Mostly Proactive	Mostly Reactive
Mostly Leads Self	Mostly Follows Others
Dares To Be Different	Mostly the Same
Extraordinary	Ordinary / Average / Mediocre
Changes the Game	Same Game as Majority

Would you agree, that without some clearly defined goals, and a time-frame of when you want to achieve them, that you are, like most other people, largely making a choice, to leave your life to chance? If you do this, you are choosing a path through life and your career, with no clear idea of where you want them to take you. A few decisions have led you to where you are now. Are you in the perfect place right now?

Don't feel bad if you feel you are not on the best path for you, most people will end on a lesser path than they would ideally like. Existing paths aren't always bad ones, some may lead you towards great things, even some extraordinary things, but for most people, by default, it leads you to an ordinary, average life, not an extraordinary one.

There are two distinct career and life choices:

1. *You work out what it is that you truly really want in the short, medium and long term, and progressively work towards achieving it. Or*
2. *You get yourself on a career and life path and just see where it takes you.*

Choice one, is being in control of your life and career, choice two is not being in control of your life and career.

I am not suggesting you work out what you really want and fix it in concrete for a lifetime, so it can never move; over time what you want might change, and also the world changes and your personal circumstances change, which might impact what is possible and not possible and also change what you want and need. You can and should, regularly review your goals, and change them if you want to.

If you distill the choice down to the essence, it is really a choice about making the most of your life, and living your life at a higher level. Isn't that really the most important thing in your life?

Often it is something bad happening, that makes people take stock and make changes, sometimes it is the loss of someone close, that provides a jolt, and a realisation that all our lives are finite, maybe it is an illness or a near death experience, that makes you think about what is really important, and where we are going. Maybe you find yourself stuck in a rut: out of work, feeling insecure at work, doing work you hate, in environments you don't like, and with other people you dislike, or perhaps working too hard for too little reward, and just feeling that your life should be better than it is.?

Are you expending lots of effort going nowhere?

Other people might see you as the poster person of success, but inside, you might be feeling terrible. You might feel anxious, stressed, worried, uncertain about your future, worried about how you can make ends meet, feeling that you are trapped on a hamster wheel, stuck in the rat race, working flat out, but going nowhere. Perhaps it might be less dramatic than these things, maybe just a feeling that you might be better off doing something completely different, breaking free from the shackles in your life, that are holding you back, or keeping you somewhere you'd rather not be. Sometimes it is outside forces that derail your perfect life, global recessions, new technologies that make your job redundant, or simply a changing world. Do you feel life is passing you by, do you see other people getting ahead, having things that you would really like to have? Would you like more time to yourself, to be doing something completely different?

Are any of these things resonating with you? Do you feel like you are ready and open for change, for a better future?

I offer you a "game change", a completely new, different and better approach to your career and life that puts you in control, and enables you to achieve the career and life of your dreams. Is that something you would be interested in? Do you want to be a leader in life or a follower in life?

Key goals that should be central to your life and should guide everything that you do

Clear Goals Need to Be Like a Compass in Your Life to Guide You

If we were to meet and I was to ask you what you wanted for your life and career, you would probably give me a long list. Fairly high on most people's list is to have a lot of money, one of the first things that comes to people's mind's if asked, "what would you want if you could have anything at all", is winning millions on the lottery; it is almost an instinctive response, but is money really the highest thing on your wish list? I've asked so many people now, what they would dream of, if they could have anything they want in their lives and their careers. Based on this, and my own understanding, I have created what I believe to be the five most significant goals for everyone, that actually encompass all the other things you might dream of, and it is these:

5 Life goals

Primary Goals:

1.   *Happiness.*
2.   *Fulfilment.*
3.   *Making a difference in the world.*

Secondary Goals:

1.   *Achieve the career success you want.*
2.   *Meeting your financial needs and desires.*

Benefits of game changing

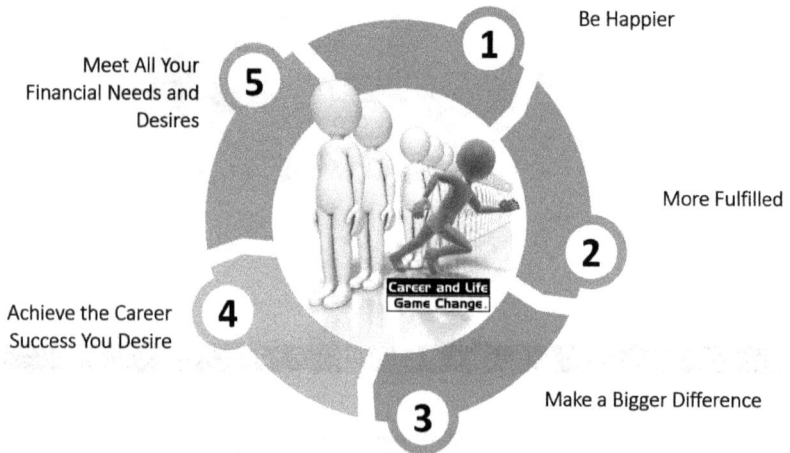

Think about anything you want, and ask yourself the question, why do you want it? You might go down a few levels, but ultimately, I believe that whatever you want can be tied into these five generic high level goals. For example, you might want to earn more money, so that you can buy yourself a lovely new house and have no debts. Earning the money enables you to meet your financial needs and desires, but it also perhaps impacts your happiness. Not only should all your desires ultimately fit into one of these five categories, there is also an interrelationship between them. If you achieve the career success you desire, you are probably doing what you love to do and are good at, and getting well paid because you are good at it, and are fulfilled because you are living your dreams, and being the person you truly are, which will make you fulfilled.

If you make these five things the primary goals in your life, I don't think you will go far wrong. I believe everything else that you might ask for would dovetail into these five. They are all actually related and it is difficult to say precisely where one finishes and another starts:

1.   Happiness

Happiness is a temporary state of joy, you can be happy being with your friends or family, doing something you love, being in nice places on sunny days etc. Happiness comes and goes. Having something to look forward to, sharing and making others happy, are all things that are likely to make you happy. It is not difficult to tell whether you are happy or not, you simply know, but happiness is scale, there are degrees of happy, reasonably happy to ecstatic with joy.

There are many things that may make you happy including:

1.   *Having fun*
2.   *Quality Experiences and Memories not just possessions*
3.   *Doing everything you want to do, when you want to, where you want to with who you want to be with.*
4.   *Quality relationships including friendships + love*
5.   *Hope*
6.   *Health*
7.   *Sharing*

8.   *Having something to look forward to*
9.   *Growth and Development*
10. *Following your hearts desire*
11. *Freedom to make choices and also having choices*
12. *Having control of your time*
13. *Having control in your life*
14. *Being healthy*
15. *Being who you really are, not who others want you to be*
16. *Living life on your terms*
17. *Meeting your financial needs and desires*
18. *Making others happy*
19. *Belonging*
20. *Loving and being loved*
21. *Caring and being cared for*
22. *Living your values and principles and ethics*

Be very clear that money for money's sake does not make you happy. I still think of the late Princess Diana, after her marriage broke up, she was beautiful, she had all the material things you could imagine, like the best designer clothes, she was admired and respected, yet you could see that she was unhappy, she lived in Kensington Palace, yet its gilded gates must have seemed like a gilded prison. She gained great solace from helping others. Supporting her charities did so much for them, but it also did so much for her, in helping her to feel fulfilled and needed. She gave so much love and kindness to others, which she must at times have been desperate to receive herself. Things can look so different from the outside in.

Some people will say you need to put career success in front of happiness and meeting your financial needs and desires, but perhaps you can't be happy if you have nothing to eat; but happiness is the goal, so earning money is sometimes a means to achieving happiness. I think the Kingdom of Bhutan has a lot to teach the rest of the world.

2.　　Fulfilment

Fulfilment is different to happiness in that it doesn't come and go quickly, it is either there semi-permanently or it isn't there at all. You can be temporarily unhappy, but still be fulfilled. Being truly fulfilled comes from being who you really are, doing what you are passionate about and love, or working proactively and positively towards it, and making a difference in the world and to others.

It doesn't matter what other people think, unless what they think, matters to you.

Tips for being fulfilled

1. *Play to your strengths – do what you are good at*
2. *Do what you love and are passionate about*
3. *Love what you do*
4. *Find your life's work and do it*
5. *Be all that you can be*
6. *Make other people happy*
7. *Contribute to a greater good – making a difference*
8. *Live life on your terms not on other people's*

Being fulfilled is being comfortable in your own skin, being who you really are in the world, and being all that you can be and want to be.

3.   Make a difference in the world

On the 14th May 2014, on brave young British man called Stephen Sutton passed away aged just 19. He has been battling cancer since he was 15 years old, but in 2013 he was told his cancer was terminal. His response to this news was to draw up a bucket list of 46 things he wanted to achieve in the near future. He set about achieving them, and inspired thousands of others with his positivity and passion for life. In just over a year, he raised £3m for charity (now nearly £4.4m) and won the respect and admiration of a nation. His story can be seen on his website: www.stephensstory.co.uk. He achieved more than most would in a lifetime; resulting in him winning countless awards, including an MBE, in recognition of his inspirational work.

Stephen made a difference and also managed to make the most of his short life. I believe he sets an example to us all.

In the modern western world, we closely identify ourselves with what we do for a living, and subconsciously we find it easy to recognise successful people. Successful people do well, they get the best grades at school, go to the best universities, get the best jobs, get promoted quicker and to a more senior level and generally speaking have the most money, the biggest houses in the best neighborhoods, the best cars, the best clothes, they can afford to buy and have the best of everything, the best education for their children, the best holidays and the best lifestyle. They are often millionaires, sometimes even billionaires, they can be rich and famous, and they get to mix with other super successful people.

From the outside they appear to have everything; the perfect lives. It is therefore not surprising that we find ourselves secretly a little bit jealous. It seems an infinitely better choice than struggling in your life to make ends meet, not having enough money, feeling insecure, pressured, stressed, worried and anxious. There seems a hugely divide between the haves and the have nots. It is therefore hardly surprising that we often find ourselves, wanting more and better. We'd secretly love to be as successful as these super successful people, and when they talk and give us advice, we want to know what they know, what they think and what they do.

Their position, status and wealth gives them and incredible lifestyle, they get to choose to do whatever they want, and everyone else wants to be with them or be like them. You'd think they would be the happiest people on earth, but they are often not. Whilst writing this book, Gerald Cavendish Grosvenor, the Duke of Westminster died aged 64. He was one of the hundred richest people in the world and the third wealthiest in the UK, according to the BBC. He said that "rather not have been born wealthy", and in 2000 he revealed he had suffered a nervous breakdown, and had become overwhelmed by depression with the pressure of running his businesses and making 500 public appearances a year. His charitable foundation donated to 1500 charities, and he served as president of the Royal National Institute of Blind People for 25 years, and president of the St John Ambulance for 10 years as well as being a Major in the Territorial Army.

Money might give you choices, but in itself it does not make you happy. We often think that winning the lottery would be the best thing that could happen to us, but Don McNay, a financial consultant to lottery winners, and the author of Life Lessons from the Lottery, has said that many lottery winners end up unhappy, divorced, broke or dead.

The belief that success = wealth, and that the ultimate success = the ultimate wealth is true if you believe that success in your life = wealth. I like what Winston Churchill said:

"We make a living by what we get, but we make a life by what we give". Winston Churchill

Difficult to believe but true to many people that winning the lottery isn't the best thing that could happen to you

A few years ago I was doing some work as a tutor for a leading business school. I got to take a group of senior executives from a leading UK bank, on a discovery learning programme, to a homeless shelter in central London near Victoria Station. To say it was awkward for the senior bankers to begin with was an understatement; eventually they ended up volunteering to work in the kitchen, preparing lunch for the homeless people, who they would normally have walked right past. In the kitchen, were a number of volunteers, the bankers were humbled by their selflessness, but one of the volunteers, candidly said "I'm no angel, I do it more for myself than I do for them". Undoubtedly his free labour was helping the charity and helping the homeless people, but the reality was, that as far as he was concerned, the benefit to him, of making a difference to others, was actually greater than the benefit the recipients of his efforts were receiving. This really points to the magic of making a difference is, the more you give, the more of a difference you make, the more comes back to you. Just look at all the super wealthy people who spent years accumulating vast wealth like Bill Gates and Warren Buffet, only to dedicate the rest of their lives to giving it away, and making a difference to others. They don't just do it for altruism, they get real pleasure from knowing that they have made a difference. I think they also see it as a moral responsibility and duty.

"The best way to find yourself is to lose yourself in the service of others". Mahatma Gandhi

Have you noticed how many people from all backgrounds and fields who gain things beyond your wildest dreams, suddenly seem more focussed on making a difference in the world, than increasing their own success. Ex US President, Bill Clinton, started the Clinton Foundation, just look at their inspiring "about us" page on their website:

"We believe that the best way to unlock human potential is through the power of creative collaboration. That's why we build partnerships between businesses, NGOs, governments, and individuals everywhere to work faster, better, and leaner; to find solutions that last; and to transform lives and communities from what they are today to what they can be, tomorrow.

Everywhere we go, we're trying to work ourselves out of a job. Whether it's improving global health, increasing opportunity for girls and women, reducing childhood obesity and preventable diseases, creating economic opportunity and growth, or helping communities address the effects of climate change, we keep score by the lives that are saved or improved.

What began as one man's drive to help people everywhere grew quickly into a foundation committed to helping people realize their full potential. Because the best thing we can do together is give others the chance to live their best life stories.

We're all in this together". Clinton Foundation

The thing is, you don't have to be rich or famous to make a difference, a kind word, encouragement, help or support of others, recognition and praise, a friendly smile, a loyal friendship all count. By all means, if you have the spare cash, donate to charities, or if you have the time or the inclination, volunteer for organisations or communities or get involved in things. It is just a case of trying to make a difference to others and the wider world as best you can every day.

There is a very interesting thing, you cannot be truly happy or fulfilled unless you make a difference to others and to the wider world. Making a difference to others isn't just some altruistic thing you have to do, it actually makes you happier, more fulfilled, more successful and helps you to meet your financial needs and desires to. If you chose to not make a difference to others of the wider world, you are actually hurting and punishing yourself. You can achieve great wealth by being greedy and selfish, conning and tricking other people, treading on them, abusing them and getting ahead at other people's expense, but you can never do these things and be truly happy or fulfilled. You can have all the wealth in the world, but with nobody to share it with, and you can end up been desperately lonely and unhappy. If you aren't a nice person and haven't earnt your money in an honest, honourable and ethical way, people will despise you, not respect you and not like you. It won't make you feel good inside, and what you need more than anything is to feel good inside.

The late Nobel Peace Prize winner, and ex-President of the State of Israel, Shimon Peres said shortly before he died: "The world, in my judgment, is divided into givers and takers. If you give, you make friends, and if you take, you are creating enemies. Nothing is costlier than having enemies."

Have you seen the film "Despicable Me", the super-villain, Gru, does all sorts of despicable things, until he meets three orphan girls, who eventually transform him into a nice guy? It doesn't matter what things you might have done in the past and regret, it is all in the past. Being a force for good in the world and making a difference, not only will make you happier and more fulfilled, but it is also likely to increase your success as well.

We all have a deep desire to feel needed, and to have a worthwhile purpose, and we can achieve that in many different ways. Making a difference to other people and the planet, doesn't just make a difference to them and it, it also helps you to feel happy and fulfilled. It is important however that your intentions are not purely selfish, or else you won't get the benefit.

Have you ever been in a situation where you've been in a challenging time and someone you didn't know, or hardly know helps you, shows you extraordinary kindness, provides generosity beyond your wildest dreams, or simply shows up in your time of need? It has happened to me on many occasions, it is the most incredible thing to receive. I'd like to say a huge thank you, to all the people who have ever helped me. It doesn't matter who you are, whether you are rich and famous or just an ordinary person, at our core we are all just the same, human beings, sharing the human experience, and everyone without exception goes through a time of need. To be in a time of need and all alone, is surely one of the worse things?

When my Dad was dying, the hospice provided the most amazing nurses to help look after him and to be a moral support to our family. I've had complete strangers offer all sorts of assistance. When I was in my early 20's having just left the Royal Navy, I spent 3 – 4 months travelling around South East Asia on my own. I was on the island of Panay in the Philippines, in the back of Jeepney on my way to the town of San Jose de Buenavista. We were on a dirt road in the middle of nowhere; this was a place that very few westerners ever visited. The guy sitting next to me started a conversation and asked me where I was going. When I told him he asked where I was going that day, when I repeated

A poor family offered me hospitality in the Philippines in 1985 when they had so little

the destination, he told me that because it was a Sunday, all transport stopped, and that I wouldn't be able to get beyond the small village that he lived in. He asked me where I would stay, I replied a guest house. He told me there were no hotels, hostels or guest houses, but that I would be very welcome to stay at his house, which I did.

They were a poor family, they lived in a simple hut with a dirt floor, there were three boulders supporting a pan of rice being cooked over a small fire. They sat me down at the table, the family all stood around whilst I was served some food. I quickly realised that they were offering me their only food, and they would have what was left over. There can hardly be much more of a selfless act than to go hungry, so that you could feed a stranger. Why is it that is often those with the least who are the most generous? What is more, I was taken to meet the Mayor and the village elders who told me I was most welcome in their village, and invited me to a party.

When it was time to go to sleep, we went to a simple wooden house on stilts, there we no beds or mattresses, we all slept on the floor together. I have travelled extensively around the world and been to

When you've got no bed to sleep on, you sleep on the floor.

many remote and far off places including the tiny island of St Helena in the South Atlantic. I get this strong feeling that we are all connected as human beings by our humanity, it feels to me that we are all distant brothers and sisters, part of the giant family, history and heritage of the human race. In the high-tech modern western world, we are ultra-connected with our advanced communication technologies and social media, but somehow, it feels to me that so many connections in the modern world are superficial, even sometimes fake and unreal. When we connect with others at a soul level, there is no hate, no discrimination, no ego getting in the way, we are all equal.

I've lost count of the times that a complete strangers have offered assistance, whether broken down in my car on the roadside, dropped something valuable and someone has come running after me. It could be a supportive email, a word of encouragement and support, maybe letting someone with a few items at a supermarket checkout go in front of you. Whether you are on the giving or receiving end, it creates a feel good factor. I believe altruism is good and should be a part of our daily lives.

Helping other people is incredibly rewarding.

4.   Achieve the career success you desire

When people first think of careers they think about jobs, but your career can be any of the following:

1.   *Employed*
2.   *Self Employed*
3.   *A Business Owner*
4.   *An Investor*
5.   *Or Supporting a Partner who is one of the above*
6.   *Doing your life's work, which might have nothing to do with money.*

Career success doesn't mean achieving the pinnacle of your chosen field, unless you want it to mean that, career success is simply being able to do and achieve and contribute as you want to. Your career success, is what you want it to be, not what others judge it to be.

Employed

Being employed is having a job and working for someone else. Typically, you are swapping time and effort and skills for money, although some people like sales people might also swap some success for money with things like sales commission. Waiters and waitresses can also earn tips for service.

A Business Owner

As a business owner, rather than being self-employed, you are selling products and services other than you. You can employ other people, and you can, if you have the customer demand, the wherewithal to deliver, and the cash flow, grow exponentially and create something that has value independent of you, that you can sell.

An Investor

As an investor, you buy assets like stocks / shares or property in the hope that you will get a return on your investment, either as income like company dividends or rent, or on asset appreciation if you sell them.

Supporting a Partner who is one of the above

You might not earn any money yourself, but you might be actively involved in supporting your partner who does, perhaps looking after the children, the home or other things.

Doing your life's work, which might have nothing to do with money.

Buddha said: "Your work is to find your work, and then give yourself to it with all you heart". Your work might not be paid work, it might be voluntary work, or even something else. Exceedingly wealthy people don't need to work, but simply managing their wealth, is itself a job, that needs to be done. There are people who inherit amazing ancestral homes, like the fictional Downton Abbey in the UK TV series, simply maintaining and preserving those for future generations is also work. Some people may have none of these responsibilities, and may in every sense appear to be people of leisure, but even their leisure can become their life's work. If you enrich yourself and pass on your wisdom, even for no feel that is work of sorts.

When you are doing what you love, and feel passionate about for your work, it doesn't feel like work at all. That is the amazing thing, you can have it all. You can often hear famous people talking about how blessed and privileged they feel, being able to do what they love, getting paid a fortune for it, and receiving public adulation.

5.   Meet your financial needs and desires

Money is important in a modern society, where things have to be paid for. First of all; you have to meet your basic needs and cover the cost of just living, beyond that, it becomes about the quality of your life, your lifestyle and the choices and freedom that money can give you, to do what you want, and to have what you want. It doesn't matter if you need or want a little or a lot, it is all relative.

Start with why?

When you are thinking about what it is that you truly want, ask yourself why it is that you want it, it will help you to realise

what is truly important and what is not. It will help you to live your life at a higher level with a greater degree of meaning and purpose behind what it is that you do.

Simon Sinek wrote a great book called "Start with why". In the book he suggests: "People don't buy what you do; they buy why you do it". If you've got good inspiring reasons why you do what you do, it will help other people to buy into you, and help you to inspire yourself.

The only way you can truly get on in the world is with the support of other people, so being more effective at winning their support will help you to achieve more. In his book The Magic of Thinking Big, Dr David Schwartz, said:

"We are lifted to higher levels by those who know us as likable, personable individuals. Every friend you make, lifts you just one notch higher. And being likable makes you lighter to lift. Successful people follow a plan for liking people."

If you have a genuine passion for what you do, you will inspire others and they will be far more likely to want to support you.

The Three Levels You Can Live Your Life At

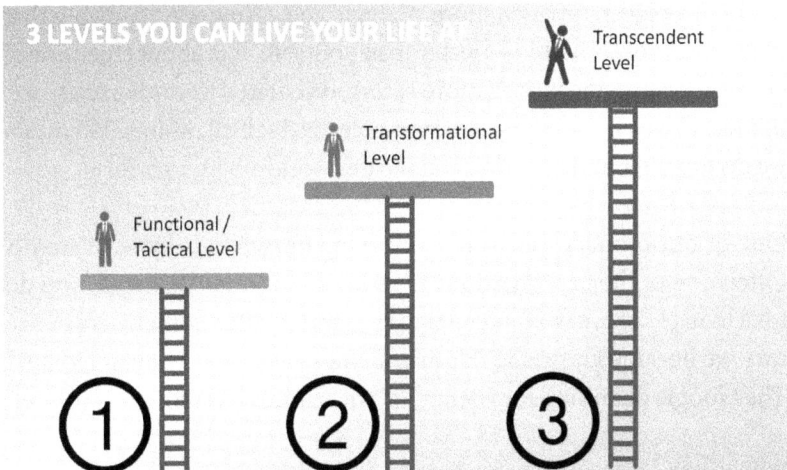

3 LEVELS YOU CAN LIVE YOUR LIFE AT

Transcendent Level

Transformational Level

Functional / Tactical Level

① ② ③

You can live your life at three different levels, if you want to achieve more and have a better life and career, consider moving up the levels.

1.   Functional / Tactical Level

The tactical level is where most people operate, for most of the time; it is about tasks needing to be completed and accomplished, to achieve direct results or outcomes.

2.   Transformational Level

At the transformation level, it is not just about tasks and outcomes, it is much deeper; it is about who we really are, how to be who we really are, how to change not just what we do, but how we live our lives, how we think and how we feel, how we see things, so that we can be wiser, achieve more, break free from convention, driving progress, positively changing the status quo, being motivated and inspired, and positively impacting others and the world. It is the level of transformational change.

3.   Transcendent Level

The transcendent Level is the highest level, it is about interacting in the world in a bigger, broader, more strategic and caring way, knowing that you are part of something greater than yourself. It is about true service at a soul level, being kinder, more caring, orientated towards excellence, not just driven by personal circumstances and selfish desires. What can we do together in the world, to make the world a better place?

One of our primary means of identifying ourselves is by what we do. Often one of the first questions we ask a stranger is: "What do you do for a living?". There is an interesting fact, and it is that somewhere in history we became known as "Human Beings", and not "Human Doings". The Google definition for "being" is "the nature or essence of a person".

What matters most, is not what we do, but who we really are, our nature and true essence. I believe that to have the life and career of our dreams we need to do nothing more than be the true essence of who we really are. When we are being our true essence, we are being our authentic, true selves; no masks, no faking it, no persona's, just the real us. I believe that when we are being who we truly are, our heads, our hearts, our souls and our bodies are all in harmony, and we hit a level of resonance in the universe where extraordinary things become possible. If you have ever read the book or watched the film "The Secret", you will have learnt about the "law of attraction", you attract into your life what you think and believe.

When we are being who we truly are at the deepest level, our motives are inherently good, and our actions are a by-product; in other words, they are a consequence of our self-actualisation. Most of our actions however come from our ego, they could be either good or bad or even neutral. As evolutionary development has given us our large brains, with the capacity for thought, learning, logic etc. we've developed our own models of reality. We humans have risen to become rulers in the world, it is a great privilege, but I believe it also comes with responsibilities, that as a whole, I feel we are only just beginning to fully appreciate.

You can live your life at any level. Different people will have different levels of consciousness, when those in power and control are operating at a low level of consciousness, horrific things can and do happen as they are today. More than ever, we need leaders and people in control to have high levels of consciousness, which will enable them to be wise.

If you can hit a transcendent state most of the time, you'll be like the Dalai Lama, if you hit it some of the time, you can be like many of the top sports people, singers, academics, engineers, entrepreneurs, and everyone who achieves extraordinary things using good energy. The transcendent state isn't limited to people perceived to be high achievers, in fact many high achievers are completely disconnected from it.

There are forces in the universe that we can't prove and can't explain. Some will deny they exist; others will have an inner knowing that they do. These forces are at play in our lives every day, we don't have to be able to see them, understand them, give them a name for them to work. If for example, you go into the world with a friendly caring approach to everyone, you are likely to receive in return friendly caring responses from other people.

What is common about people who achieve extraordinary careers and lives is that they have frequently have powerful dreams that drive them. Have you ever been in a concert with a singer, who is in their zone, singing from their heart, there is an energy that radiates from them, that can impact everyone that is there and millions of people around the world. It can cheer them up, make them cry, make them smile. Energy and emotion has impact. When a sports person achieves their greatest goals, most other people can feel the energy and feel inspired. I am sure there have been many people who have inspired you in your life. The term inspired, is according to the late bestselling author and guru Dr Wayne Dyer, , similar to "in-spirit", which is the feeling of connection to something bigger than ourselves.

I believe that you have just as much capability as anyone else to connect to your higher self, to achieve personal transformation, and even transcendence.

CHAPTER 6

TAKE CONTROL OF YOUR LIFE

"Taking control of your life and career means being able to see both holistically and recognising the interdependence between them".

Become The Author of Your Life Story, Script Writer and Director of Your Life Movie and CEO of Your Life

To game change your career and life, you first need to make a conscious decision and commitment to become, the author of your own life story, the script writer and director of your own life movie and the CEO of your own life.

The key idea is that you decide what you want in your life, and you turn it, not just into a goal and an objective, but make it an imperative, in other words "not a should", but something "that you must do, no matter what". How often have you said "I should do this or I should do that", but then haven't done it, e.g.. I should lose some weight, I should get fit and do some exercise, I should each healthy food? There is a big difference when something becomes a "must", because there isn't an option to not do it. I must breathe or else I'll die.

There is a saying, "be careful what you wish for", there is a big danger of wishing for the wrong things. Imagine having the equivalent of the genie in the story of Aladdin, who says "your wish is my command", you can have whatever you want, all you need to do is to decide what. Remember to be specific, because whatever you ask for you are going to get.

Imagine for a moment you are very old, and you go to the cinema to see your own life movie. You get your bag of popcorn, the safety curtain comes up, the lights dim and your life movie starts to play, what are you going to see? Are you going to sit there bored, embarrassed, wishing you'd written a better story, or are you going to be full of tears of joy, of the wonderful life you have had?

The important thing to realise, is that if you don't like the movie of your life, it is too late to change it, you can't change the past, but you can change the future. Every day, we all go to our bank account of time and make a withdrawal, a day is a day for all of us, we've all got exactly the same amount of time in a day, it is down to each of us, to decide what to do with it, and how to spend it.

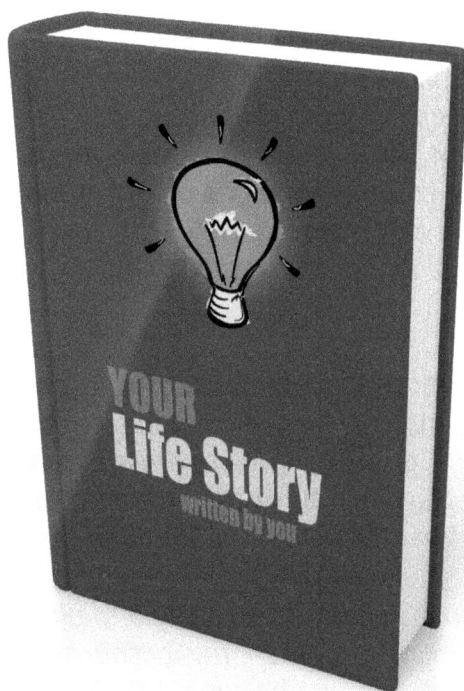

Imagine for a moment, the most terrible thing; you go to a meeting with your doctor after you've had some tests, and he or she tells you the devastating news that you've probably got a year to live, possibly two if you are lucky. What happens then, to how you think about spending your time? Every day counts doesn't it?

I have heard many stories of people being told they are going to die, feeling intensely alive, and gaining clarity on what is really important. On searching the internet for examples, I came across an article written by Oliver Sacks, who was a doctor, a best-selling author, and a professor of neurology at the NYU School of Medicine, who died in 2015. The New York Times has referred to him as "the poet laureate of medicine." He was a bright and wise man, who wrote some words of wisdom titled "my own life" in the New York Times on 19th February 2015. In his words, he touches on so much that this book is all about:

"It is up to me now to choose how to live out the months that remain to me. I have to live in the richest, deepest, most productive way I can. Over the last few days, I have been able to see my life as from a great altitude, as a sort of landscape, and with a deepening sense of the connection of all its parts. This does not mean I am finished with life.

On the contrary, I feel intensely alive, and I want and hope in the time that remains to deepen my friendships, to say farewell to those I love, to write more, to travel if I have the strength, to achieve new levels of understanding and insight.

This will involve audacity, clarity and plain speaking; trying to straighten my accounts with the world. But there will be time, too, for some fun (and even some silliness, as well).

I feel a sudden clear focus and perspective. There is no time for anything inessential. I must focus on myself, my work and my friends. I shall no longer look at "News Hour" every night. I shall no longer pay any attention to politics or arguments about global warming.

This is not indifference but detachment — I still care deeply about the Middle East, about global warming, about growing inequality, but these are no longer my business; they belong to the future. I rejoice when I meet gifted young people — even the one who biopsied and diagnosed my metastases. I feel the future is in good hands.

I have been increasingly conscious, for the last 10 years or so, of deaths among my contemporaries. My generation is on the way out, and each death I have felt as an abruption, a tearing away of part of myself. There will be no one like us when we are gone, but then there is no one like anyone else, ever. When people die, they cannot be replaced. They leave holes that cannot be filled, for it is the fate — the genetic and neural fate — of every human being to be a unique individual, to find his own path, to live his own life, to die his own death.

I cannot pretend I am without fear. But my predominant feeling is one of gratitude. I have loved and been loved; I have been given much and I have given something in return; I have read and travelled and thought and written. I have had an intercourse with the world, the special intercourse of writers and readers.

Above all, I have been a sentient being, a thinking animal, on this beautiful planet, and that in itself has been an enormous privilege and adventure".

Dr Oliver Sacks 1933 – 2015

Your career and life mission control

Imagine taking the red pill again, only this time, rather than arriving in Planet Earth Headquarters, you find yourself in another truly extraordinary space, which is very similar, but this place is much smaller, but equally impressive. In big letters over the entrance is a huge sign; in big bold letters it clearly says "Your Full Name – Career and Life Mission Control".

As you walk through the entrance lobby into the dimly lit mission control room, you are reminded of NASA's Mission Control Centres, that became famous in the early days of space exploration, used in the Apollo Missions to the Moon, but this mission control room, reflects today's technology. Gone are the banks of CRT computer monitors, with teams of people, and in its place, a cathedral sized hall, dimly lit with stylish modern LED lighting, and a giant wall with ultra-high definition displays, that are so big, you can imagine they must be projected and ultra-high resolution they are so clear.

Perfectly positioned in the centre of the room is a cluster of seating, and in the centre raised higher on a platform is the coolest chair you have ever seen. This is clearly meant for you and you get a distinct sense that its location is not only central to the room, it is central to your career and life.

To the side of the chair is the same touch pad display that you saw the Planet Earth Chief Executive using. The display is so clear and so intuitive; you feel like you instantly know how to use it. Very quickly, you start to access the same things that the Planet Earth Chief Executive was showing you about your own life. Every second of every day of your life has been recorded in high definition, only this time you are looking at your life from the outside in, not the inside out. You discover that you can view every situation from every imaginable perspective. You can see the big picture of every situation and the detail as well, you can see it from other people's perspective.

It reminds you of a computer game, only everything is real, the real you, real people, real situations. For some reason, rather than being spooked about the whole situation, you feel perfectly calm, rather than seeming strange, it feels like you've been here before, that you belong, that you just know why you are here, and all the reasons are good and positive. You instinctively know you can't change the past, it is history, but you can change the way you perceive it, you can see things in a new light. You can use your imagination to project scenarios into the future, but you know that the future is just a model, you won't change the future in

Stages of Life.

your mission control room, you'll only change it in the real world, by what you see and perceive, what you think and what you do.

You can access life expectancy information on this website which draws from World Health Organisation statistics and others sources: ***https:// en.wikipedia.org/wiki/List_of_countries_by_life_expectancy***. On average, women live longer than men. Life expectancy varies dramatically depending upon where you live, at the time of writing this book the lowest life expectancy was for men in Sierra Leone whose average life expectancy was just 49.3, with the highest life expectancy being females in Japan with an average life expectancy of 86.8. To help you to see where you are in your life journey you can complete a simple career and life planning tool that will help you to see where you are. This is available on the following website: ***www.FeelGoodChangeTheWorld.com***

Life and Career Planning Report For:

Jonathan Blain

Date of Birth 24-04-1963

Age: 53 years 5 Months 15 Days

Gender: Male

Nationality: United Kindgdom

Average life expectancy for Male in United Kingdom is 79.5 Years

Click Here to See National Life Expectancy

Click Here to See National Retirement Ages

You Hope to Live Until the Following Age: 85 year(s)

National Retirement Age: 65 year(s)

you Hope to Retire at Age: 65 year(s)

Started Your Career Ages: 17years 4 Months 6 Days

You Have Been Working For 36 Years 1 Month 9 Days

According to the National Retirement Age you have completed 75.78% of your career (36 Years 1 Months 9 Days) and have 24.22% remaining (11 years 6 Months 15 Days)

According to Your Desired Retirement Age you have completed 75.78% of your career (36 Years 1 Months 9 Days) and have 24.22% remaining (11 Years 6 Months 15 Days)

According to statistics from the World Health Organisation, which states currently live expectancy for male in United Kindom is 79.5 Years, you have 32.68% of your life remaining (24 Years 11 Months 15 Days).

According to your own personal estimate of your life expectancy 85 yeras, you have 37.11% of your life remaining (31 Years 6 Months 15 Days).

Career and Life Plan Assuming National Retirement Age and National Life Expectancy

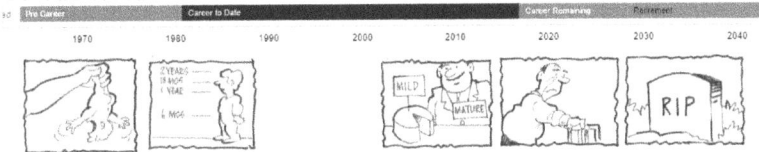

Pre Career	Career to Date				Career Remaining	Retirement	
1970	1980	1990	2000	2010	2020	2030	2040

Career and Life Plan Assuming Your Desired Retirement Age and Your Estimated Life Expectancy

Pre Career	Career to Date				Career Remaining	Retirement		
1970	1980	1990	2000	2010	2020	2030	2040	2050

Get Free Life Planner Report Now: FeelGoodChangeTheWorld.com

A fairly obvious place to start planning is to see where you are on your life journey. Whilst none of us know how long we will live, we can start to make some assumptions and consider a range of options. It can be eye opening to see how much of your career and your life you might have left , it focuses your attention on how precious your life time is. If you don't seize the day, today and really try and take control of the rest of your life, when are you going to do it?

Carpe Diem - Seize The Day

Don't hope for a miracle, choose to take control of your own life. You can only live your life today, so make each today count and your life should become a collection of good days!

As you explore the mission control system, you see that you can access the most incredible displays, that are projected in high definition onto the wall in front of you. You can change the displays in an instant, it is like being able to build a giant dashboard about every aspect of your life and career.

Sitting in your own life mission control room, gives you the opportunity to think about what is important to you and what isn't. The logical thing is to make changes in your life, to prioritise that which is important over that which isn't, and that is most important, over things that are less important. This is a simple, but highly effective strategy.

If you accept that your primary life goals should be happiness, fulfilment and making a difference, imagine a dashboard display of these things being projected onto your mission control room wall. Just how happy and fulfilled are you, and how much of a difference are you actually making? I know it is a rhetorical question, but if you want to take the way you live your life and manage your career to the highest level you need to know how you are doing. None of these things are binary, it is not just a case you are happy or unhappy, fulfilled or unfulfilled, there is degrees of everything, levels of happiness and fulfilment. You have to decide what is right or wrong for you, and you can use the Blain Change Framework ™ to help you to reassess things.

NASA didn't put a man on the moon without a vision, a strategy, a plan and resources; each mission had a mission control centre, where every facet of the mission was controlled. There is a saying: "you are only as good as your weakest link", the secret is to try to ensure that you either don't have any weakest links, or that you ensure that each link in your success, your life or your career is up to the job, so that it doesn't fail. Most people hardly manage their life and career, they rarely if ever have a career and life plan that they can articulate and stick to. Creating one, forces you to think about who you really are, what you really want and how you can get it, and enables you to monitor your progress and make changes if necessary.

The make a difference revolution

We often hear people talking about the importance of making a difference, it seems obvious, but do we really know what it means, or indeed why it is so important?

"You can make a difference positively or negatively"

Instinctively we think about making a difference, as a positive thing. Imagine a football / soccer match, and your team is losing, nothing your team does seems to work, that is until the coach pulls you off the substitute bench in the last ten minutes. You are energised, motivated and inspired; you lift the spirits of your team, you give them belief in themselves and courage, that they were lacking. Reinvigorated, together you turn the match around, score three late goals and win. Before you came on the pitch the team was losing, but after you came on, you made the difference, and turned a losing situation into a winning situation. Perhaps you scored the goals, or maybe you didn't. This is a great outcome, another scenario is that your team were winning, you were pulled off the substitute bench, you played appallingly and your team lost, arguably you made the difference between winning and losing and in this scenario the difference you made was a negative one. Perhaps we should use the term "making a positive difference".

"Making a difference is doing more than is considered normal or expected of you."

Making a difference usually relates to an impact on something you do to other people, or other things. If you recycle your rubbish, or walk to work rather than using your car, you probably are making a positive difference to the planet, and to other people. If you help a colleague who is struggling at work, you help them, but you also help the organisation.

It is easy to think that the benefit of making a difference goes just to the person or thing who has had a difference made to it, but the reality is, that making a difference is just another form of giving, and ultimately and perhaps counter-intuitively, giving is more rewarding than receiving. Many of us, will perhaps have experienced the joy of being given a gift as a young child, but we will probably remember the joy was often relatively short lived. Our lives are richest, when we give or share with others, or where we make a difference to other people or other things.

According to the mindful word website:

"Academic research and thousands of years of human history confirm that achieving meaning, fulfilment, and happiness in life comes from making others happy, and not from being self-centred."

I'd like to propose a revolution that I believe can change the world, and that you can be a part of. The essence of this revolution is that we are all way more powerful than we think we are, and that lots of small things, added together can make a huge difference, indeed small things on their own, rather than being a drop in the ocean, that doesn't make any difference, can create a ripple that changes the world. Just think of the impact of Martin Luther King's words in his "I have a dream speech"? Rumi, a Persian poet and Sufi master was born 807 years ago in 1207 and said: "You are not a drop in the ocean. You are the entire ocean in a drop." The simple truth is that you matter, and you can make a difference. It is a bit like the Butterfly Effect, which is all about cause and effect, the idea being that it is possible for a butterfly flapping its wings in New Mexico to cause a hurricane in China if it flapped its wings at a particular point in space and time. If you cast a stone into the water, the ripples that emanate from the splash continue long after the stone has fallen to the bottom. You can create ripples in the world, that can have a profound effect. Just look at the impact that some young YouTubers have been able to create vast followings of millions when they started with none whatsoever, from the confines of their bedrooms.

It is easy to feel powerless, yet simple choices that you make, that can seem so small and so insignificant, can make a massive difference.

Set yourself the goal of every day doing simple easy to do things that make a difference to others, to the environment, or to the wider world.

I bought a Fitbit step counter when I wanted to lose some weight, by simply measuring the calories I had used up and the number of calories I had consumed, setting a daily deficit. Doing this I managed to lose 2 stone in 2 months. I also joined a group of similar aged people who shared the number of steps they had done, which gave me a useful benchmark to help my motivation. My idea is to take a similar principle and apply it to making a difference, simple daily goals that are really easy to complete which might include:

1. Random Acts of Kindness, Consideration, Help and Encouragement
2. Generosity of Spirit
3. Maximising the Quality of Human Interactions
4. Deliberately Making Other People Feel Significant and Good
5. Doing something for the environment, community or wider world
6. Proactively supporting and encouraging others to make a difference
7. A smile
8. Greeting people rather than just walking past them
9. Using other people's name
10. Having impeccable manners
11. Doing something for the planet

12. Not doing something that causes harm
13. Writing letters of support and encouragement to those in leadership positions.

CHAPTER 7

AN
INNER
JOURNEY

"You need to gain a deep understanding of your true identity to figure out what you really want, which means you are then left with one job of working out the best way of getting what you want".

At face value it might seem like working out who you really are is a ridiculous thing to do. After all, you have been you all your life, surely you don't need to expend any time, effort or expense working out who you really are, do you?

One of our primary means of identifying ourselves is by what we do. Often one of the first questions we ask a stranger is: "What do you do for a living?". There is an interesting fact, and it is that somewhere in history we became known as "Human Beings", and not "Human Doings". The Google definition for "being" is "the nature or essence of a person".

What matters most, is not what we do, but who we really are, our nature and true essence. I believe that to have the life and career of our dreams we need to do nothing more than be the true essence of who we really are. When we are being our true essence, we are being our authentic, true selves; no masks, no faking it, no persona's, just the real us. I believe that when we are being who we truly are, our heads, our hearts, our souls and our bodies are all in harmony, and we hit a level of resonance in the universe where extraordinary things become possible.

When we are being who we truly are at the deepest level, our motives are inherently good, and our actions are a by-product; in other words, they are a consequence of our self-actualisation. Most of our actions however come from our ego, they could be either good or bad or even neutral. As evolutionary development

Watch Out For Ego

has given us our large brains, with the capacity for thought, learning, logic etc. we've developed our own models of reality.

Famous People Before They Were Famous

Please don't hold me to the accuracy of the following facts, they were obtained with some internet research, and we all know everything on the internet is not true, but this is what the research said rich and famous people did before they were rich and famous:

1. Sean Connery was once in the Royal Navy, a milkman delivering milk door to door, a truck driver, life guard and coffin polisher.
2. Kanye West once folded clothes in GAP
3. Walt Disney was once a paper boy and worked for the railroad selling travellers snacks and magazines.
4. Johnny Depp was once a telemarketer.
5. Madonna worked as a showgirl in France and at Dunkin Donuts.
6. Angelina Jolie did a course in mortuary science.
7. George Clooney was once a shoe salesman and a hand on a tobacco farm.
8. Jon Bon Jovi once worked as a janitor.
9. Sandra Bullock was once a waitress and a bar tender.
10. Harrison Ford once worked as Boy Scout adventure camp as a counsellor.
11. Jennifer Aniston once worked as a telemarketer.
12. Jim Carrey once worked as a janitor at a factory.
13. Michael Fassbender was once altar boy at weddings and baptisms.
14. Oprah Winfrey was once a grocery store clerk.

When you are not where you want to be in life, you can think of yourself in terms of what you do now, where you are now, and what you have now. The truth is that you can do different things in the future, you can be in a difference place, and have a lot more than you have right now.

You are a far greater person than you most likely think you are, you are capable of more than you could imagine; there is true greatness in you, because there is true greatness in everyone.

to be fired, in fact, the guy I took over from, suggested firing him was probably one of the first things I would need to do. I was told that he was not only incompetent, but he had a terrible attitude as well.

He was working on my worst, most run down station, that was waiting to be knocked down and rebuilt. What I discovered however, was someone completely different who was highly talented, highly motivated, with a brilliant attitude. By the time I left, he was no longer running the worst station in my area, he was running the best, and furthermore, he was able to achieve the biggest promotion that anyone had ever achieved in the company of over a thousand people. If I had told him, when I took on the role, what he would achieve, I am sure he would never have believed me, because I don't think then, that he truly believed in himself or that it was possible. I saw something in him, that he didn't see in himself to begin with. I might have given him some encouragement and a chance, but he did the hard work. He chose to bring the best of himself to work every day, to make a difference and to go the extra mile, and the results were spectacular. He subsequently went on to become a COO in the industry.

None of us, know what we have inside of us, and what we are capable of, unless we have the courage to find out, to put ourselves on the line, to go past our comfort zone and to try, and when we sometimes fail, which we inevitably will, to pick ourselves up again, learn the lessons from the failure, and try again. When we stretch ourselves, we step out our comfort zone and it is hard, but when we continually do it, it becomes the new normal and gets easier, which gives us the ability to stretch that bit further again.

It really comes down to a chance, some encouragement, a belief in ourselves and stretch. It is really a question of one step at a time, one challenge at a time, one lesson at a time. It is so easy to give up, to either never believe in the first place, or to stop believing, and to start making excuses, like: I'm not good enough, it will never work, it is not possible for me, I am not smart enough, life is not fair etc. Whether you think you can, or whether you think you can't, you'll most probably be right.

When I was an Area Manager for the Mobil Oil Corporation, running a group of Petrol / Gasoline Stations in North West London, there was a trainee manager, who was on performance warnings, and was just about When Gary Dutton left school at 16 with no qualifications, from a poor home, his teachers said he would never amount to anything, but now he is one of the richest and most successful people in the UK, and has been awarded an MBE by the Queen for Services to Industry, and has donated hundreds of thousands of pounds to charities. His colleagues and competitors mocked him originally, but he was better than them. If others mock you, or think that you'll fail, or that you are not up to it, that is their business; use other people's negativity to make you more determined to prove them wrong, and use others motivation, encouragement and belief to make you stronger and more fearless as well.

If you are feeling stuck, frustrated, worried, dissatisfied, unhappy, unfulfilled, depressed, or down and out, your self-esteem, self-confidence and self-belief is likely to be low. Don't make the mistake of under-estimating yourself. It might be tough, it might be challenging, you might be running on empty, but it is always possible to turn things around. Often when you are in a highly challenging situation, you can see no way of changing your situation, but where there is a will, there is nearly always a way.

I've learnt the hard way that the greatest challenge we all face is to achieve a higher level of consciousness about everything, life, the world, the universe, careers etc. but also a consciousness about ourselves. An enlightened friend of mine, Rex Barker, says: "Can you tell me who you are? Not your name, your roles, or your stories but who you really are?" When we try to explain who we are to others, we instinctively go to our name, our roles and our stories. We think these things are us, and at one level they are, but it is at our persona / ego level; which is the model of ourselves that we perhaps believe and portray to the outside world and to ourselves, but it is not the magnificent beings that we all are at our core. Imagine asking the celebrities mentioned who they really were when they were younger and not rich and famous, what might they have said? Equally if you ask them who they are now, you might get very different responses. Richard Gere is a very famous A List celebrity actor, he is the sort of person who has the red carpet rolled out for him, people want to have their pictures taken with him and have his autograph. He is looked up to, put on a pedestal, invited onto TV shows, given the best tables at restaurants, and invited to the best parties. What many don't know is that he is also a humanitarian activist, at the time this book was written, he has worked on behalf of the homeless for more than 10 years. He made a documentary type film called "Time Out of Mind", where he posed as a homeless person, sat at street corners for up to 45 minutes at a time and rummaged in bins for food, slept on benches, and begged for spare change. No one recognised him, and most people ignored him. He said "It was bizarre." "As long as I was in character, I could see people from two blocks away, making a judgment based on how I was dressed. I was very visible to them. People are afraid of being sucked into a black hole of failure and misery. But then it touches something deep in all of us. None of us are that secure that it couldn't be us also."

We've all got feelings and emotions, thoughts, dreams, beliefs, hopes, fears, strengths, weaknesses, things that make us happy and things that make us sad. We have some common traits, but we can be different in different ways. It is like we are all actors in the play of life, but often we are acting a life that is fake, behind the persona, we can be

We Have Feelings

someone different. Knowing your identity is knowing your authentic self, and when you are your true authentic self in the real world, where

your persona is the real you, you are likely to be happiest and most fulfilled. When we live a lie, when we try to be who someone else wants us to be, it creates incongruence, pressure and stress. It is like a gay or trans-gender person pretending to be someone they are not, it is enough to make them seriously unhappy, depressed even suicidal. Our mission in life should be to be who we really are, as Abraham Maslow described as self-actualised, not only being who we are, but being all that we can be and want to be. Being who you really are in the world is freedom, being someone you are not is like imprisonment. Often we get so used to playing out the persona, that was often educated into us by others, that we lose the real us, we have no idea who we really are. Our perception of who we are is often so masked by our roles and our stories, that we don't even see it. Discovering your true self, is one of the most liberating things you can do.

When I was going through a challenging time, a friend introduced me to a coach and a psychometric assessment tool. It was definitely a landmark moment in my life, not only was I able to take a quantum leap in terms of understanding myself better, but I also was able to take a quantum leap in terms of understanding other people and how we human beings interact, communicate, work together, value each other etc. A lid was lifted on a world of self-understanding and human understanding, that I didn't know existed. Discovering that other world, was like a personal enlightenment, it took the way I looked at myself and others, to a whole new intensely deeper and more profound level, with life changing possibilities.

As I sat here writing these words, my very good friend Erling Gudmundsson called from Iceland. It made me think about the science fiction novel "Journey to the centre of the earth" by Jules Verne. The story was based in Iceland and involved intrepid adventures descending into a volcanic crater and journeying towards the centre of the earth, making incredible discoveries. I thought it made a good analogy with taking an inner journey of discovery to the core of who you really are, so that you can the answer the simple question that my friend Rex Barker asks: "who are you really"?

You have to know your true identity to know what you truly want

One of the most profound discoveries I ever made, was that we need to know who we truly are, to know what we truly want, the two things are intrinsically linked. We might think we want certain things, when in fact we don't. The essence of who we truly are, is a combination of all our parts, our head, our heart, our soul and our physical bodies. Buddha said: "Your work is to find your work, and then give yourself to it with all your heart". To best find your work, you need to find the real you. For over two decades, I have been studying how best to do this, and without doubt, I believe the most effective way is to use a portfolio of different assessment tools, both psychometric and others.

I'd like to give a big warning about assessment tools, some of them are good and others are not. Just because an assessment tool says something about you, doesn't mean that it is true. Many knowledgeable people have however spent years creating ways of assessing human beings in meaningful ways, and validating the accuracy of the assessments. Different assessment tools are able to identify different characteristics and attributes, to the extent to which I personally was amazed. If you do an assessment and largely agree with it, and the people who know you, and even those who don't, agree with it also, and your past and current behaviours are in line with it, you can believe that the assessment is largely true. They will never be 100% true or accurate, but they can be accurate enough to be extremely useful. I now have a massive folder of personal assessments.

Sometimes people will use an assessment tool and say "that is not me", when those who know them, know that it is. We all want to have the good assessments that portray us in a positive light, but it is an absolute fact that we all, without exception, have strengths and weaknesses, that is natural and normal. Often our greatest strength can in certain circumstances be our greatest weakness, e.g. someone who sees themselves as a natural leader, go getting who makes things happen, will see these attributes in an entirely positive light, but to someone else on a bad day these attributes might come across as bullying, domineering and arrogant. We naturally tend to think that people like us are good and people who are the opposite perhaps are bad, or certainly not as good as us, but the truth is that the world needs everyone.

Things that you are bad at, other people will be good at, which means we all need to be in the right roles in life, which is why Buddha said: "Your work is to find your work" and then "give yourself to it with all your heart". Knowing your true identity helps you to find your work. For some people it is easy, they have already found it, and it was easy to find. My lovely wife Jenny, always knew she wanted to work with children from the earliest age, she left home aged 16 to do a two-year nursery nurse course, she loved it, excelled at it, and has done ever since. Seeing someone do what they are destined to do, who has found their life's work is like poetry in motion, you can feel it and sense it. If you ever watch TV programmes like the X Factor, you can sometimes see someone whose life's work is to be a singer, it is sight to behold, it can put a lump in your throat and a tear to your eye just watching and listening to them, sometimes even the judges are in tears, and the audiences are on their feet.

If my wife Jenny found her life's work easily, discovering mine, has been the exact opposite, I've found it incredibly hard, I've been completely attached to roles and stories like so many people are, and I've had plenty of both, which has made it even more confusing. From the earliest age, I wanted to be the author of my own life story, director of my own life movie. I used to want the exciting, rewarding and adventurous life that I saw other people having in the movies, yet that desire came often from my ego and the persona I had created for myself. I struggled to find or recognise the real authentic me, it has taken me over half my lifetime to work it out, and I feel what a waste in so many ways. It is part of the reason that I have written this book to help other people to make the most of their life, and short cut that inner journey to discover who they truly are, and what they are meant to do to feel most alive, most fulfilled and most rewarded.

Discovering who you truly are is an epiphany moment, that can change your life forever. Knowing who you truly are, enables you to discover what you truly want, which leaves just one task of actually doing what it takes to get it.

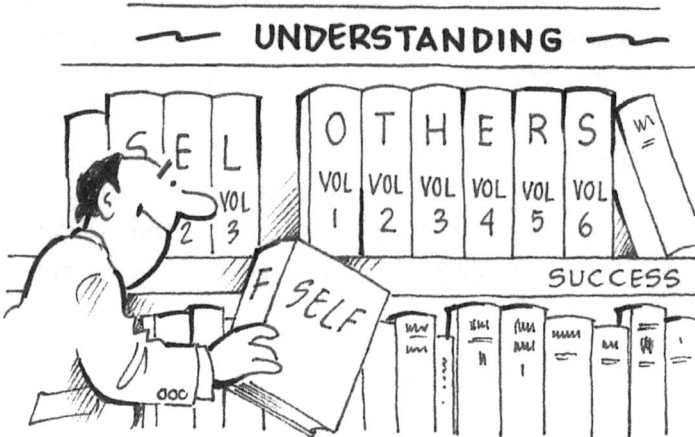

Some assessment tools appear to be really comprehensive, so much so, that you could think tell you everything you need to know about yourself, however, I have discovered that taking a raft of them fills the gaps, provides increased detail, and also provides the opportunity to cross reference for consistency. Using different assessments tools, is like gaining a 3D perspective on yourself. The truth is that we all look different from different perspectives, and are different in different circumstances. We are complex beings, and there are many nuances to our identity.

Many assessment tools provide very useful graphical representations of data, or pithy bullets of information that are clear to understand.

Some address very specific issues, and others are more general in their nature.

Many have very useful categorisations, that mean you can articulate who you are to others in a common language, and with evidence. Many assessment tools are able to differentiate between the conscious you and the persona you show to the world, and the sub conscious, real authentic you, that lies inside you. It becomes incredibly easy to be able to see your strengths, weaknesses, ideal areas of work, ideal work environments, roles, motivational factors, learning styles etc. Your performance in particular roles can be predicted with a fair, almost spooky degree of accuracy.

Even though we are all completely different human beings, there are human characteristics that can be defined, which apply to some people and not to others. Some people for example will love to stand up in front of a big audience and give a presentation, whilst others would rather die than have to do that. Some people will love detail, others will hate it. Some people are natural risk takers, others are incredibly cautious. There will be some roles like entrepreneurs where risk takers are needed, and others where risk takers would be disastrous. You wouldn't like to be on an plane with a pilot who enjoyed taking risks, or have anyone responsible for your safety who was careless and lax. There are sayings, "horses for courses", "square pegs in square holes, round pegs in round holes". The truth is that there are an infinite number of different shaped and sized holes and pegs, you just need to be doing things in your life that are perfect for you.

CHAPTER 8

MAKING THE GAME CHANGE

"The time comes when you have to make the decision to break free from the herd and live your live your life and manage your career at a higher level, so that you can make the most of your life, and make the greatest difference."

Feel Good
Change The World™

We are living in the most extraordinary time in the history of humanity, where we are balanced on a knife edge between great opportunity on one side, and potentially catastrophic crises on the other: economically, politically, socially, environmentally and individually. Now is a perfect time to wake up to the reality of where we are collectively as humanity, and also where you are personally.

The career and life game change, starts with choosing to game change the way you live your life and manage your career, so that you can make the most of your life, and be happier, more fulfilled, make a bigger difference, achieve the career success you want, and meet your financial desires.

The career and life game change system is designed to address something of utmost importance, literally a matter of life and death; to be precise your own life and death. What can be more important than your own life? On the one hand, we will typically fight to save our lives, to stay alive, because we don't want to die, but on the other we are discovering that many people, in ever increasing numbers, are choosing to commit suicide and die, rather than simply existing with no quality of life. Quality of life is everything, yet many people are suffering huge unhappiness and lack of fulfilment, caused by numerous challenges, issues and problems that need to be addressed. These challenges can affect anyone, rich or poor, young or old of one faith, nationality or another. Life today is frequently complex and pressured.

Change and break free from the herd

To game change your career and life to make them better, you need to change the following:

1. *The way you see things e.g. See things differently.*
2. *The things and way that you think e.g. Think differently.*
3. *What you do e.g. Act Differently.*

Exactly what you need to see, think and do differently depends upon who you are, your circumstances, and what everyone else is doing. These things are likely to continually change, therefore you need to be prepared for continual change as well. Most people will do broadly the same things; by having the courage to break free from the herd, to be original, different and better, you can gain advantage, and achieve extraordinary results and outcomes. Most people will never try to leave the herd, they would rather follow the herd off the edge of a cliff than have the courage to choose better paths, we instinctively feel there is safety in numbers, but often there isn't. This approach to life doesn't seem logical, until you consider our upbringing and psychology that makes us want to fit in with the majority, and the allure of taking the easiest path, not the best path is massively strong. We are also so typically risk averse and afraid to fail, that we don't have the courage to take risks and to trust ourselves, and our ability, and good judgement.

Take a holistic perspective and proactively manage your career and life

Most people don't proactively manage their entire career and life from a holistic perspective; by doing this alone, you can be one step ahead, and increase the chance of having both a better career and a better life. By taking the way you manage your career and life to the highest level, you can maximise the chance of achieving the best outcomes.

When you take the way you live your life and manage your career to the highest level you need to know:

1. *Who you really are?*
2. *What you really want?*
3. *How you can best get what you want?*

Be who you really are

You have to know who you really are to know what you really want

Who you really are and what you really want are flip sides of the same coin, the two are intertwined. Often who we think we are, isn't who we truly are, and what we think we want, often isn't what we really want. It is only when you consider what makes you, you, that you recognise the complexity of who we all are, made up of four parts that are often difficult to distinguish:

1. *Our head – the thinking logical part of us.*
2. *Our heart – the feeling and emotional part of us.*
3. *Our body – the physical us*
4. *Our soul – the spiritual essence of ourselves, that is difficult to prove exists, the part of us where our true identity and highest-self resides, the part of us that is connected to the natural world and all living things, where our deepest emotions and values emanate. Awareness of souls is*

linked to our levels of conscious-ness. Some people will be largely disconnected from their soul energy, whilst others will live their lives around it. To live your life at the highest level you will need to discover connections to higher purposes and deeper levels of enlightenment.

Orientate your life and career around what is most important

You have to know who you really are to know what you really want

Most people will subconsciously orientate their lives and careers towards surviving and then thriving, with thriving being defined the way most people define success, as rising to the top in your chosen career and earning more and more money, being looked up to by others. Generally speaking the more money people earn the more successful they are considered .

Under the career and life game change system, the goals are changed as follows:

3 primary goals:

1. *Happiness.*
2. *Fulfilment.*
3. *Making a difference.*

2 Secondary goals:

1.   *Achieving the career success, you want.*
2.   *Meeting your financial needs and desires.*

I am not suggesting that money isn't important; it is difficult to be happy if you are starving and don't have anywhere to live, but money is not the end objective, happiness, fulfilment and making a difference is. Orientate your life towards the achievement of these things and you'll increase the chance of making the most of your life and achieving the best quality of life. The best things in life, the truly priceless things, don't cost money.

Increase your consciousness

To enable you to see, think and act differently, you need to gain increased consciousness, and start to see the big picture as well as the minutiae of things. If you do this, you are likely to recognise that the quality of your life is a combination of what you give and also what you get. You might start off with a wish list of things that you want, without realising that giving is both a duty and an obligation as a member of the human race and as a custodian of the world for future generations, as well as one of the very best ways of being truly happy and fulfilled.

Consciousness is key to a better life and a better world

Embrace a new enlightenment

The world is in need of a new enlightenment, based on the three tenets of:

1. *Wisdom*
2. *Love*
3. *Imagination*

Embracing these things into your life, will enable you to not only make a bigger difference, but it will help you to live your life at a higher level with a greater quality of life, and greater happiness and fulfilment.

Choose to live your life at a higher level

You get a choice to live your life at one of three levels:

1. *Transactional level, the lowest level.*
2. *Transformational level the next highest level, and*
3. *The transcendent level, which is the highest level.*

Know why now is a unique time in human history

Which level you choose to live your life at, will to a great extent, depend upon your level of consciousness, and your connections to the whole of humanity, and the whole world, and everything within it. When your consciousness increases you will recognise that you are living in an extraordinary time in the history of humanity for three primary reasons:

1. *Exponential growth in the global population.*
2. *Exponential progress and advancement.*
3. *Exponential rate of the doubling of knowledge.*

Recognise that humanity and the world are on the knife edge of crisis

The world and the whole of humanity are on a knife edge and precipice of great opportunity on one side and also great threats on the other:

1. *Economically.*
2. *Politically.*
3. *Socially.*
4. *Environmentally.*
5. *Individually.*

Develop a deep curiosity and go on an inner journey

By exploring, developing a curiosity, and going on an inner journey, you are likely to see the bigger picture in great detail and with much appreciation, and also the finer detail in great depth, which passes over most people's heads. Doing these things will bring you to a greater self-understanding; an understanding of the meaning and purpose of your own life, and a realisation of what you need to do to maximise your happiness, fulfilment and the difference you make to others and the wider world. When you put some of your existing knowledge, beliefs and understanding through the Blain Change Framework, you may discover things that you thought were right, that were actually wrong, things that you thought were good that were bad, things that you thought were impossible that were possible and vice versa etc.

You might feel powerless, but when you game change your approach to the way you live your life and manage your career, you can discover the immense power you have and the genius that lies within you.

Put everything on the table that can help you and overcome the barriers and blockers

When you game change your approach, you put everything on the table that can help you; the only restrictions are that whatever you do must be legal and ethical. In essence you do the things that are likely to help you to achieve the life and career of your dreams and stop doing things that are preventing you from

achieving those things. The biggest barriers, preventing you from achieving the life and career you want are internal ones of:

1. *Fear*
2. *Guilt*
3. *Criticism*
4. *Resentment*

You'll discover that unlocking your potential is as much an inner game as it is an outer game in the real world. The following self-related issues that impact your quality of life that might need to be addressed are:

1.   Self-Belief and Confidence

Self-belief and confidence is all about developing a certainty: about:

> Who you really are
> What you really want
> Your values
> How you are going to achieve your goals and gain the confidence that you will indeed actually achieve them.

If you have self-belief and confidence, you believe: "I can do it. I will do it. I will succeed and achieve my goals".

Believing you can do it, and you are capable of doing it is really important to your wellbeing.

2.   Self Esteem

Self-esteem is believing that you are worthy of everything that you want, and everything that you have, and that you are more than fine just as you are.

Valuing yourself.
Seeing yourself as important.
Believing you and your life matters.
Seeing yourself as equal to or more important than others

3.   Self-Image

Self-image is about how you see yourself; your perception about yourself.

Good self-image is seeing yourself positively. Bad self-image is seeing yourself negatively.

4.   Self-Understanding and Awareness

Self-understanding and awareness is knowing who you are, and what makes you who you are.

5.   Self Respect

Self-respect is about living your life according to your values, so that you can be proud of who you are.

6.   Self Improvement

Self-improvement is about how you grow, develop and improve yourself.

7.   Self-Efficacy

Self-efficacy "is the extent or strength of one's belief in one's own ability to complete tasks and reach goals". Wikipedia

8.　　Self-Love

Self-love is essential for a happy life, yet large numbers of people don't love themselves and the consequences can be devastating.

Self-love is essential for a happy life, yet large numbers of people don't love themselves and the consequences can be devastating.

Work on your life and career not just in them

When you start to work on your life and career, not just in it, in just the same way that successful business owners and entrepreneurs work on their business, not just in it, you can fast track to solving problems and creating and seizing opportunities, it is like putting one foot on the accelerator of a car, whilst taking your other foot off the brake, that you didn't even realise was on it. Gaining increased consciousness will enable you to see the situation you are in, from a new enabling, positive and holistic perspective. Understanding yourself at a deep level, is probably the most significant thing you can do. It also helps you to understand others and your place in humanity and the wider world. By taking a holistic approach, you get to look after the whole you, maximising your wellbeing, the quality of your life and the contribution that you make.

Invest in yourself

Game Changing your career and life, requires initial up front effort and investment, in exactly the same way as a sports person wishing to compete and win at the highest level, invests in themselves and does the hard work. The biggest initial investment is in the inner journey to discover who you really are and what you really want, this is largely a one off exercise, once you get that deep level of understanding, it largely lasts you a lifetime, and your focus can then shift to doing the things in the real world that will help you to get and give what you want. The ten step process you need to follow to achieve this is relatively logical.

10 Steps to Specifically Achieve the Career and Life of Your Dreams

Step 1	Make the choice to take control and become a leader in life.
Step 2	Work out who you really are and document it.
Step 3	Work out what you really want and document it.
Step 4	Reality check what you want with the real world and come up with final goals.
Step 5	Create a strategy of how you are going to achieve your goals.
Step 6	Translate your strategy into plans you can implement.
Step 7	Take action.
Step 8	Measure results.
Step 9	Make improvements and changes as required.
Step 10	Repeat the process on a regular basis.

1

Make the choice to take control and become a leader in life

The truth is you are either in control of your life and career, or you are not in control of your life and career.

To be in control of your life you need to be a "leader in life". To be a leader in life you need to know what you want for your life and career for the short term (next 12 months), medium term (1 year to 5 years), and long term (5 years +). Having worked out what you want, you need to turn those wants, into clearly defined and written down goals. Once you have your goals, you need to spend every day working to achieve them, until you do achieve them.

The Career and Life Game Change System™, is based on you making the choice that you want to take control and become a leader in life? If you make this choice you need to find ways of holding yourself to account, or else you will go back to your old ways. Change is always hard to begin with, but becomes easier over time.

Your biggest risk, is that your decision to take control and become a "leader in life", could very easily become like a, new year's resolution, that lasts a few weeks and gets forgotten, or a dieter that starts dieting and then quits, or someone who starts to give up smoking and then quits.

Making the decision to take control and become a leader in life, must be a one-way ticket, with no going back. A very good friend of mine, John Peck, (www.John-Peck.com) at 59 years old, decided he wanted to row the Atlantic Ocean in a race from one of the small Canary Islands La Gomera across to the Caribbean. The cheapest way to fly to La Gomera was to buy a return air ticket. When he arrived in La Gomera for the start of the race, the first thing that he did was to tear up his return air ticket, and commit to his decision, and after months at sea, he finally made it.

Make a commitment to change course and stick to it

If you decide to make the choice to take control of your life and become a leader in life, to achieve the career and life of your dreams, and in particular the following:

1. *Increase your happiness.*
2. *Increase your fulfilment.*
3. *Increase the career success that you desire.*
4. *To meet all your financial needs and desires.*
5. *To make a difference in the world.*

You need to tear up your metaphoric return ticket to your old ways. Rowing across the Atlantic Ocean was far from plain sailing, deciding to take control and to become a leader in life isn't going to be all plain sailing or easy either, but the prize is likely to be worth it.

Extraordinary achievements require extraordinary effort, ordinary, average, mediocre achievements, require ordinary, average, mediocre effort, you have to decide whether you want to be a leader in life, or a follower in life. The choice is yours.

2

Work out who you really are and document it

Having decided you want to take control, become a leader in life, and set out to achieve the career and life of your dreams, the next steps are best done together. Step 2 is working out who you really are and documenting it and step three is working out what you really want and documenting.

The best way of working out who you really are at the deepest level is to invest in a portfolio of different assessments. I've got a folder nearly 4 inches thick with mine, which helps to give me a greater self understanding than anyone else I know. I have found it to be incredibly useful and beneficial.

In the late bestselling author Stephen Covey's book, Seven Habits of Highly Effective People, which has sold over 10 million copies he outlines the seven steps of highly effective people:

1. *Be proactive.*
2. *Begin with the end in mind.*
3. *Put first things first.*
4. *Think win / win.*
5. *Seek to understand, then be understood.*
6. *Synergise.*
7. *Sharpen the saw.*

I recommend you adopt these habits.

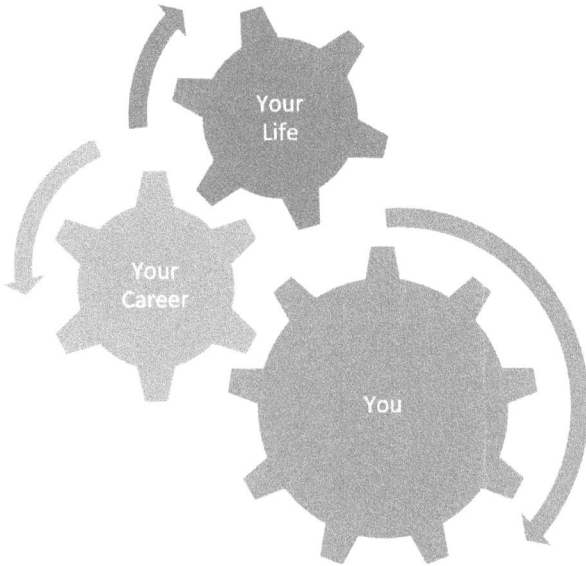

Habit number two is begin with the end in mind. With this you need to work out what the career and life of your dreams would look like for you. If you don't have a goal / objective, you don't know where you are heading, you wouldn't know if you'd arrived. It is vitally important you are crystal clear on your goals; woolly / vague goals are useless. When the objective is the life and the career of your dreams, the key element is "your". It is all about you, so the starting point has to be a deep dive into you.

Your career and your life are two different things, but they are closely related. In Stephen Covey's book, habit number six is synergise, which is really about creative cooperation with others. However, synergy is useful when considered in relation to:

1. *You.*
2. *Your Life.*
3. *Your Career.*

The definition of synergy in dictionary.com is: "the interaction of elements, that when combined, produce a total effect that is greater than the sum of the individual elements". Your career is a subset of your life, it can help you to create the income and wealth to meet your financial needs and desires. What you choose as a career depends upon many factors including what you like, and are passionate about, what you are good at, qualified and experienced in, and what is available and possible for you to do.

There is a great quote from Buddha: "Your work is to find your work, and then give yourself to it with all your heart". There are two fundamental ways of looking at you're your career:

1. Your career is just about earning money, so that when you are not working, you can be doing what you want to, having the lifestyle you desire. Or

2. Your career is more than being about earning money, it is a part of your life purpose, your life's work, your contribution to something greater than you, it is something that you love to do, that makes you feel, alive, energised, excited and passionate.

3. With option one, your life becomes a treadmill, work becomes something to be endured:

4. Being a leader in life means choosing option 2; if you've got a terrible career that makes you really unhappy it is going to ruin your life. You need to find a career that gives you everything, that you like and feel passionate about, that you are good at and that suits who you really are.

Knowing who you are at every level including the very deepest level is essential to enabling you to achieve the career and life of your dreams. You might be thinking to yourself, I've been me all my life, of course I know who I really am. I used to think this, until something happened. I was running a business that was going through a challenging time. Someone I knew suggested I get myself a coach to help me to move through those difficult times, which I did. The coach introduced me to a psychometric profiling tool, that literally changed my life. I spent ten or fifteen minutes completing an online assessment too. The result was a 38-page report, that started with a two-page overview all about my personal style, that described me in great detail with 33 different sections / categories, covering things like my strengths, weaknesses, ideal working environment, my value to the team, my blind spots, my learning styles etc. It also managed to come up with some fancy charts showing the different energies that lay within me, with descriptions of what they meant and separated my sub-conscious self from my conscious-self etc. At that point, I realised how little I actually knew about myself. The accuracy of the report was simply unbelievable; it enabled me to not only understand myself, but to also understand other people. In terms of increasing my self-understanding, I'd say I experienced a 100% increase, probably even more.

I was so struck with the power of the assessment tool; I undertook very expensive training to become a licensed practitioner.

As human beings, we are like onions, with lots of different layers. I subsequently discovered many other equally impressive assessment tools that each present information about you in different ways.

When you know yourself well, you get to learn about the different elements that impact your happiness, your fulfilment, your career success and ultimately your income and wealth.

Getting to know yourself at the deepest level is essential to enable you to achieve the life and career of your dreams, doing this is like finding pieces of a jigsaw and putting them all together, which enables you to see the complete picture.

You have to be able to see what you are and what you are not, what suits you and what doesn't suit you, what you are good at and not good at. You need the right information to be able to make the right decisions.

Assessment tools and some focused coaching can help you fit the pieces of the puzzle together in the quickest and most effective way.

Get to know yourself at the deepest level

Achieving the life and career of your dreams is as much about going on an inner journey as it is going on an outer journey in the real world.

Work out what you really want and document it

Step 2 and step 3 are closely aligned, they are really two sides of the same coin.

Given that you comprise of four elements:

1. *You head / mind. (Your Thinking)*
2. *Your heart. (Your Feeling / Emotion)*
3. *Your body. (Your energy, your confidence, your ability to physically do things etc.)*
4. *Your soul / spirit. (Your connection to a higher purpose & something greater than yourself. Your universal knowing).*

You need to make and align your goals to all of these things. Your head might be saying you are best to get the highest paid job, but your heart might be feeling that would make you really unhappy.

In May 2011, a poor farmer called Susyono in Indonesia had been bemoaning his lot in life. The following night he had a dream where a guy with white hair said he wanted to give him a golden puppet, but that there was a price to pay. As well as farming Susyona used to collect rocks that he sold to builders. Something made him think about looking for gold. He did and he found some, and then some more, and then even more. To begin with, only he and his friend new about it, but after seeing their crops unattended, and a new fridge and children playing games on mobile phones, the village chief discovered their secret. Soon everyone was looking for gold, not just local people, but people came from far and wide. Soon there were disputes, the work was dangerous and many people had accidents and some were killed. Large smelters moved in from outside, and soon the tropical paradise was ruined, the landscape was scarred with mining activity. Mercury that was used in the process contaminated the ground and animals and it went into the water and fish, soon people started to get ill, women miscarried their children and some were born with birth defects. Eventually Susyono felt so uncomfortable with how he was earning the money, he gave it up and set up a small store.

How you earn your living matters, more money in itself doesn't necessarily make you happier, if you sell your soul and don't care about the environment and other people, you are unlikely to be fulfilled or happy, so be careful what you wish for.

You need to know what your life's work is going to be, sometimes it finds you, but other times you have to go looking for it.

What you need to do is to come up with a two lists, one for your life and one for your career of what you dream of:

1. *Having and*
2. *Achieving and*
3. *Doing and*
4. *Being*

For both your life and your career, in both the short (next year), (medium (1 yr. – 5yrs) and Long (5yrs +) terms.

Think about what will:

1. *Make you most happy*
2. *Make you most fulfilled*
3. *Represent the career success you desire*
4. *Be your financial needs and desires*
5. *We the way you can make a difference and make a contribution to a greater good.*

4

Reality Check what you want with the real world to come up with final goals

You might decide you want to be President of the United States, but if you weren't born a United States Citizen, you are not allowed to be President. You might think you want to be a rich and famous pop singer, but if you are tone deaf and have no talent for singing, it might be a tough thing to achieve.

You might set your heart on a career path that is in serious decline where there are no job vacancies and likely to be even less need for those skills in the future.

PRESIDENT OF THE UNITED STATES

ASSISTANT MANAGER

Be realistic about what is possible for you and what isn't

I am into sailing, I once had a yacht that was moored in the centre of an estuary, I got a lift out to it in a motor boat with the intention of sailing to the nearby quayside where I was due to meet a friend. I cast off the mooring, and started to sail towards the quayside, after a short while the wind died completely, the yacht stopped moving, and the tide which was running out the harbour, started to carry me back to where I had come from. By luck I was able to catch the mooring buoy, but with no engine, I couldn't go anywhere. The hours went by, and with no mobile phone my friend got worried and eventually sent out a rescue boat to find me stuck on my mooring. There are times in the world where the tide turns, and what used to be easy, becomes hard, if not impossible. Sailors always try to use the tides to their advantage, that is what you need to do in your life and career. I used to be a Royal Naval Officer, and I have the equivalent of a ships driving license. I was once sailing across the Atlantic Ocean in a giant ship HMS Fearless which featured in the 1977 James Bond film, The Spy Who Loved Me, as the ship which picks up Bond's escape pod. The ship was 520 foot long and 12,120 tons, the bridge was approximately 80 foot from the sea level. We went through a hurricane with steady 120 mph winds and mountainous seas, all we could do was to steam into the storm. We had revolutions on for 18 knots, yet all we could manage was 4 knots over the ground. Even when you are really big, you can't fight the forces in the world.

You might think, that if the circumstances of the world, means you can't achieve the career and life of your dreams, then that is it, that it is impossible. Whilst that particular dream might be impossible, if you are resourceful and tenacious and look hard enough you will find something that is even better.

Knowing what you want, depends knowing what is possible, to know that, you have to be an explorer and go searching for what is possible and also become an innovator and create what doesn't already exist.

There is nothing more infuriating than setting your heart on something that becomes out of reach for any reason, but it happens sometimes.

It is vitally important you don't waste your life aiming for goals that are simply never going to be achievable. There is a conundrum with this however, in that what many people thing is impossible, is actually possible Being extraordinary means seeing, thinking, and acting differently to other people, and doing extraordinary things, that ordinary people think is not possible. There is no easy solution to this, you have to use your judgment.

"Whether you think you can or whether you think you can't you'll be right". If you truly believe that something is possible then it probably will be, but if you genuinely don't believe something is possible then it almost certainly won't be for you, and you shouldn't waste your time trying.

5

Create a strategy of how you are going to achieve your goals

With stage 4 completed you will have your written set of goals for your career and your life in the short, medium and long term, what you have to do next, is to devise a strategy of how best to achieve your goals. A strategy is what do to achieve a goal, and a plan is how you will do it.

Your goals could be very different from other people's, in terms of a career, your choices for earning a living and creating income and wealth are:

1. *Employment*
2. *Self-Employment*
3. *Being a Business Owner*
4. *Being an Investor*
5. *Supporting a Partner Who Earns a Living*

To be a leader in life, you need to dare to be different. To meet your specific goals you will need to choose the best strategies, there are however some generic strategies that should be relevant almost whatever your goals.

To Game Change You Approach to achieve the career and life of your dreams is to take control. You do that by deciding to lead in life and not follow, work out who you really are and what you really want, reality checking it against what is possible in the real world.

At this point you should be significantly ahead of followers in life who have done none of these things.

The thing about being a game changer is that you need to:

1. Raise your expectations.
2. Raise your standards.
3. Start at the Leading edge of whatever you are trying to do, then innovate to improve.
4. Take whatever you are doing to the highest level
5. You need to embrace positive change by using some of the following suggestions:

a. **Change the way you see things – Become an Explorer**

1. Change your perspective including putting yourself in other people's shoes.
2. See the big picture.
3. See the small picture, the minutiae and the details.
4. See beyond other people's horizons.
5. See what could be, rather than just what is today.
6. Learn to see the value in yourself.
7. Learn to see the value differential and difference between you and others.
8. Look for opportunities and be prepared to seize them.
9. Look for threats and be prepared to defend yourself against them.
10. Develop foresight, have a continual forward facing radar.
11. See your life and career in relation to other people, organisations and the wider world.
12. Always look for opportunities to add value to things,
13. people and organisations.

b. **Change your thinking – Become an Innovator**

1. Be open minded.
2. Be curious.
3. Use your imagination.
4. Use your judgment.
5. Be ahead of the game not behind the game.
6. Anticipate what might happen.
7. Be alert to changing situations.
8. Be a lifelong learner.
9. Play to your strengths.

10. Make sure you find ways of staying motivated and inspired.
11. Think like a leader.
12. Continually grow and develop
13. Do more things that increase your chances of success.
14. Do less things that decrease your chances of success.
15. Play to your strengths.
16. Do things you are passionate about.
17. Live your life and run your career by a set of principles and values.
18. Keep your integrity in tact at all times.
19. Have good reasons why you do what you do.
20. Try to make it easy for others to like and support you.
21. Treat other people in a better way than you would like to be treated yourself.
22. Develop courage of your convictions.
23. Go on an inner journey.
24. Invest significantly in your career and life management.
25. Continually seek wisdom and build your own personal library of wisdom.
26. Join the dots, take knowledge and skills from one area and apply it to another.
27. Seek to fail quickly and move on if you do and learn from your experience so you become stronger.
28. Discover what works best for you and stick with it.
29. Always look to make a difference.
30. Focus on small improvements, that may on their own not seem that important, but when added together can make a big difference, in fact can make all the difference.
31. Always look at things from a cause and effect perspective.

32. Try to see things at a deeper level to see beyond what most people see, i.e. see the politics and games, and motivations that are in play, hidden meanings, hidden agendas.
33. Continually look for leverage that you can use to get advantage and results.

c. **Change what you do – Become and Adventurer**

1. Do more.
2. Do new things.
3. Do Better things than other people.
4. Be a pioneer and innovator and try out new things.
5. Develop skills in advance of actually needing them.
6. Develop win / win relationships.
7. Dress for success.
8. Stay fit, healthy and not overweight if possible.
9. Make a point of always thanking people, and try to always find positive things to say.
10. Get yourself a coach and the best one possible even if you are already supremely successful.
11. Continually try new things.
12. Push for progress, advancement and improvement.
13. Always use people's names.
14. Face your fears and overcome them even if it is difficult.
15. Do everything to build your self-confidence.
16. Do everything to increase your self-esteem.
17. Overcome limiting beliefs you might hold.
18. Move from operating at a transactional level to a transformational level and even to a transcendent level.
19. Do right by other people.
20. Have empathy and emotional intelligence.

21. Be good at introducing yourself to others.
22. Build powerful strong, useful personal networks and give to other people by a factor of at least 2:1 e.g. give more than you expect to receive back.
23. Use leverage to make things easier.
24. Be resourceful and tenacious.
25. Be your true authentic self every day.
26. Be the best of yourself.
27. Keeping pushing yourself to be even better.

It doesn't matter what you want for your life or your career, it is how you go about getting what you want that matters. There are many different ways of achieving goals, in fact there are as many different ways as innovative people. You need to see your life and career as a game that you play. You could liken it to a sport. If you care about winning, (winning for yourself), you need to do what the most successful sports people do; you use every resource available to you, and work on every factor that can increase your success, providing it is legal and ethical. When you are playing a game of sport, you think the people with the best skills in that sport are going to be the ones who win, but counter intuitively, other factors may be responsible for making the difference between winning or losing.

In sport these could be things like, fitness, attitude / mind set, diet, nutrition, sleep, happiness, belief, psychology, strategy etc. You just need to apply these thought processes to your life and career.

A number of years ago I made, what I believe is still the world's most comprehensive video based education programme on leadership excellence, where I interviewed top leaders from different walks of life. One of the people I interviewed was Michael Wilson, who founded a company called St James's Place with a few friends, and grew it to at UK FTSE 250 company, in fact, the company even made it to the top 100 companies in the UK for a while. He said that he would far rather taken someone who was competitive and into sport than he would people with high academic credentials like MBA's. Having a Pit-bull determination and resolve to succeed is one of the most powerful potent strategies you can adopt.

Believe that there are multiple strategies possible, imagine a warehouse full of different strategies that you can go to, and use as tools and resources, to achieve your goals, quicker and more effectively, and to make as big a difference in the world as possible. Be continually on the lookout for new strategies that you can use. Sometimes a strategy works for a while and then stops working.

6

Translate your strategy into plans you can implement

Failing to Plan is Planning To Fail

If a strategy is about what to do to achieve a goal, a plan is about how you will do it.

A strategy is an idea; a plan is about how that idea, translates into tasks / actions that need to be completed and resources that need to be used.

The best way of translating a strategy into plans that can be implemented is to use a project / task management tool to create a project plan.

There are many of these available, some need to be paid for like Microsoft Project, others are free like: freedcamp.co, producteev.com, ganttproject.biz, meistertask.com, 2-plan.com, asana.com, trello.com, bitrix24.com and many more.

7

Take action

Nothing happens unless you take action, you've got to implement your project plan, the surest way to get nowhere is to do nothing, you quickly revert to being a follower in life.

Tips for taking action:

1. Be organised.
2. Measure twice cut once, so you don't waste time with unnecessary mistakes.
3. Get up an hour earlier than you need to, do 20 minutes of exercise, twenty minutes preparing for the day, and 20 minutes learning or studying something that will help you grow and develop.
4. Set yourself a schedule of tasks and try to always keep ahead of schedule, such that you never fall be-

hind schedule.

5.   Do a monthly, weekly and daily plans as well as short, medium and long term ones.

6.   Set yourself milestones and give yourself treats.

7.   Always try to do more than other people expect of you, to a better quality than they expect and quicker than they expect.

8.   Consider outsourcing certain tasks, get others to help you in your life and career. These days it is extremely easy to get a whole variety of different people to do different things for you, from doing your washing to cleaning your house, to researching for jobs or for helping you if you are self-employed or a business owner.

9.   Establish routines so you can make the most of your time.

10. Consider buying audio books so you can listen to them in otherwise dead times, like when you are commuting to work, doing the shopping, the housework, going for a walk, whilst driving on a car journey.

Measure Results

The reason for having objectives and goals is so that you have something specific to aim for and so that you know when you have achieved what you were setting out to achieve.

You've got to use your common sense in terms of the records you keep. I highly recommend that you use a project management / planning tool, to record completed tasks. There are plenty of paid and free ones available on the Internet.

It can be a huge motivator seeing how much you have accomplished, and feeling you are on a path to achieve the career and life of your dreams.

Make improvements and changes as required

The only thing you should set in stone are your principles and values, so that you ensure that everything that you do is ethical, so no matter what else, you can sleep well at night on that front.

You must change your goals and objectives as soon as you either achieve them, or feel that they no longer properly reflect what you truly want. Also your goals are a moving target, at the beginning of the year for example, your short term goal is the next 12 months; by the end of the year, you should have completed your goals, and your new short terms goals become the next 12 months. If you are not making the progress you'd like, you should be able to see it in your task manager and in the lack of results. You can motivate yourself by continually looking for better ways to achieve your goals.

You need to adopt of personal strategy of continual and never ending improvement, that way you make your life as easy as possible, always taking the path of least resistance, providing of course it is the most effective way of achieving your goals. You also need to look for leverage wherever you can, so that you use the least effort to achieve the greatest things.

You need to make the most of your time, and get the right work / life balance, so you don't work yourself into an early grave.

10

Repeat the process on a regular basis

The Golden Gate Bridge in San Francisco USA is a famous bridge. People often speculate how often it gets painted, the truth is that it is painted continuously. Managing your career and life isn't something you do as a one of exercise, it is not even something you do every now and again, it is something that you need to do continuously, because you change, what you want changes, and circumstances change. The painters of the Golden Gate Bridge don't paint the same place every day over and over again, they do it in sections. You need to do the same thing with managing your life and career.

AFTERWORD

Congratulations on reading this book, and taking steps towards making the most of your life, and making a bigger difference in the world.

This book has clear themes in it, that relate to a fundamentally new game changing way of living your life and managing your career, that is designed to help you to be: happier, more fulfilled, make a bigger difference, achieve the career success you want, and meet your financial needs and desires.

Did you notice recurring themes that were threaded through this book? Has it woken you up to the reality of your own life, and the situation the world is facing right now? This book is a tool designed to trigger an ah ha moment, an epiphany that changes everything, and a personal transformation, that enables you to feel better and make positive changes in your life. It is also designed to support the formation of a new movement based on the ideas in this book; better lives, being a force for good, with a deep desire to make the world a better place for everyone and everything. Do you want to join?

Getting the message the book contains, is only half the challenge, putting what you have discovered into practice, taking the way you live your life and manage your career to the highest level, and effecting changes that make the difference to you, to others and the wider world is the hardest part.

You may very well find yourself agreeing with the contents of this book, but most will not make the changes they need, to get the benefits that they desire. I wish this was not the case, but I know the power of conformity of doing what the majority do, is exceedingly strong, and that faced with an easy option and a harder option, most people will go for the easier option.

The likelihood is that you'll opt for the easy option, doing what everyone else does, and maintaining your own status quo, but I hope you are one of the few.

AFTERWORD

If however, you are one of the exclusive few, you'll feel a deep desire to change, a connection to your soul, and a knowing that you are going to make the shift, and do whatever it takes to be happier, more fulfilled and make a bigger difference. You know it will be harder, but you know that you have to do it.

You may feel excited about the prospect of moving forward, of moving beyond the challenges and frustrations of your existing situation. You'll feel that you read this book for a reason, and that reason was to act, to raise your game, the quality of your life, and the contribution that you make to others and to the wider world.

You might also feel that this book tells you what you already knew, and that you are already living your life at a higher level, or have started on a pathway to do this. If this is your situation, you might be excited about the prospect of connecting with other like minded people, recognising the interdependence between us all, and the truth that when we discover synergy and opportunities for win / win collaboration, extraordinary things become possible.

You may need to read this book again and again to get the deeper messages that underpin it, and the connections to your own situation, and your own life, that make it extra relevant for you personally.

I'd like to personally thank you for taking the time to read it. If you enjoyed it and got a lot from it, I'd be grateful if you could tell your friends and others you think might benefit from reading it, and please spread the message far and wide. Your contribution can make a huge difference. Thank you.

I'd also be pleased to receive your feedback and hear your stories and your thoughts, that I may share with others. You can email me: jonathan@FeelGoodChangeTheWorld.com marking the subject title "Feedback" and also be sure to connect with me on Facebook.

NEXT STEPS

Feel Good
Change The World™

We can only ever live our lives today; the past is history, and you'd be crazy to try and live your life in the past, and when tomorrow arrives it will be today.

If you try to always live for today, whilst lining up your tomorrows to be as good as possible, you are unlikely to go too far wrong.

Simplicity is always best, so think of a good life as comprising of a lifetime of good days. All you have to do, is to achieve one great day at a time.

This book contains some powerful messages, that you'll either get or you won't. If you don't get them, then nothing can change, however if you do get them, then you've got a simple choice: 1. Carry on the way you have been or 2. Decide to change the way you live your life and manage your career forever, following the advice and guidance in this book and specifically the steps outlined in chapter 8.

Go to:
www.FeelGoodChangeTheWorld.com

1. Get your free life and career planner report.

2. Join the Feel Good Change The World Movement.

3. Consider joining the Feel Good Change The World Accelerator Programme.

4. Book a Power Hour Conversation With Jonathan Blain.

ABOUT JONATHAN BLAIN

Jonathan Blain is a pioneer, visionary and extreme game changer on the GC Index and C-Me Profile. He fits a definition of a "Purple Squirrel", combining an inexhaustible well of creativity and imagination, with more traditional director and implementer skills.

Positioned at the leading edge of progress, human endeavour and enterprise, he helps people to:1. Live better lives, 2. Have better careers, 3. Run better businesses / organisations and 4. Make the world a better place and: achieve more, be more, do more, have more, know more and make a bigger difference.

A life of extreme highs and lows has given him humility, and transformed him into a servant for humanity. With the capability to change landscapes and move the human race forwards, Jonathan is a catalyst & driver of change, he transforms the future. He has created the world's most comprehensive video based leadership education. He offers new ideas, new thinking and new solutions.

He is married with three daughters, and lives in Henley on Thames in the UK. He loves travel, meeting people and anything to do with the water, yachting, sailing and adventures.

He is a Bestselling Author of 13 Books/$3.8m+ sales, on Business / Entrepreneurship, Selling, Technology (8 Books on SAP / Goldmine CRM), Careers etc. He is also a Thought Leader, Philosopher, Speaker, Problem Solver, Improvement Specialist. Versatile Interim / Consultant / Leader / NED / Entrepreneur / Intrapreneur. Ex Royal Navy Officer, CEO of Quoted Plc + MD of FTSE 100 Subsidiary.

——— ABOUT JONATHAN BLAIN ———

His work has previously been endorsed by many top leaders including nine heads of UK top 1000 companies including: Apple, Sony, St James's Place, Carphone Warehouse, The Director General of the Institute of Directors, the First Sea Lord of the Royal Navy, and one of the co-founders of software giant SAP.

In everything that Jonathan does, he looks to make a difference, challenge the status quo, push for progress, make things better, create & exploit opportunities, & achieve extraordinary things. He has emotional sensitivity and can inspire and uplift people.

Speaking + Consulting + Senior Executive Coaching

- Jonathan is available to speak at events worldwide.
- He also runs many programmes and events globally. See web sites for details.
- He undertakes a wide range of consultancy assignments.
- He is a regular contributor / guest in the media.
- He coaches senior executives, entrepreneurs and high net worth individuals and also helps them to write books.
- He offers 1:1 Power Hour Phone Consultations and Face to Face Meetings. Go to www.JonathanBlain.com for more details.

ABOUT JONATHAN BLAIN

Connect With Jonathan

jonathan@jonathanblain.com

www.facebook.com/jonathan.blain.12

@jonathanblain

www.linkedin.com/in/jonathanblain

JonathanBlain.com

Book a Power Hour Consultation With Jonathan
www.JonathanBlain.com

ACKNOWLEDGEMENTS

I'd like to thank everyone who has helped me whilst I have been writing and creating this book, in particular the following people:

Thea Tagulao
Thea has typeset this book. At the time this book was written, she was a young lady from the Philippines, who was studying Advertising Management, whilst simultaneously developing her skills in photography, layout and graphic design. She also took on the role as photographer for her university's newspaper. Thea's involvement in the book is proof of the globalised world in which we now live. Thea has shown maturity above her years, great professionalism, and has committed whole heartedly to creating the best book possible. As far as I am concerned, she is a great role model, who has made the difference to this book project. She has been a fantastic team member, who has really cared about our team objective, to help people to feel good and make the world a better place.

Will Lankston Adam Jarvis, and Paul Lockyer
Will has been in charge of a pioneering identity business called ArkHive, and Adam and Paul are Identity Experts, who have been managing the UK's first Identity shop, in Henley on Thames in the UK, which is where I live. There was a business centre at the identity shop, where I've done some of my writing. Will, Adam and Paul have been great sounding boards, and all have given me honest feedback and encouragement as I've developed my ideas and content. Even though their involvement in identity is more related to proving who you are to employers, banks, landlords etc. I have felt there has been synergy with this book, which explores our own personal identity, and how a deep level of knowledge of that, can help you to make the most of your life. The free coffee was greatly appreciated!

ACKNOWLEDGEMENTS

Irfan Idrees
Irfan has brought expertise and experience to the book design process and has helped polish it for printing and e-book distribution.

Paul Barclay
Paul came up with the splash writing for my logo. He is a very talented artist, illustrator, designer and sign writer. His awesome Paul Barclay Brand is on the ascent: www.PaulBarclayDesigns.com.

If you happen to be in Dartmouth in the UK, I suggest you visit his shop and studio in 1 Oxford Street and mention my name!

Simon Chance
Simon has been my best friend since we were nine years old; he is like a brother to me, and we have been on many adventures together. His friendship and support, continually reminds me how important friendships are in our lives. Good friends are priceless, they make life worth living, it is great to have them, but also we need to remember that we need to try to be good friends to others too.

My Family
Finally I'd like to thank my entire family for their love,support and understanding. The creative process is rarely straight forward, and they have had to put up with me working long hours to bring this book to fruition.

SPREAD THE WORD

I hope you've enjoyed reading this book and that it can be a catalyst to you feeling good and positively changing the world.

In my experience if you've read something that has moved you, it is nice to talk to other people about it. Whilst this book is intended to be simple, it is difficult to fully explain it in a sentence or two.

I'd like to suggest that you consider buying a copy of the book and giving it to your family, friends, colleagues or others in the hope that it might benefit them too.

How often in life, has someone told you about something and you have not acted on it? Buying a copy of this book for someone else is an act of love and kindness, and it is also a way of perpetuating the positive peaceful revolution that is behind the Feel Good Change The World Movement™.

If somebody else gave you this book as a gift, why don't you consider doing the same thing to someone else.

Together we can all Feel Good, Make a Difference and Positively Change The World.

Best wishes,

Jonathan

INDEX

Index

Symbols

4Afrika Initiative 62–284

A

Abraham Lincoln 44–284
Abraham Maslow 183–284
Adam Jarvis 276–284
Ahmed Djoghlaf 87–284
Aids 96–284
Aladdin 210–284
Albert Einstein 44–284
Aldicarb 162–284
American Independence 139–284
Amy Winehouse 22–284
Andrea Leadsom 84–284
Angelina Jolie 225–284
Apollo 14 144–284
Argentina 161–284
ArkHive 276–284

B

Bankers 81–284
Battle of Waterloo 139–284
Bee 163–284
BHS 70–284
Bill Clinton 197–284
Bill Gates 71–284
Bird Flu 96–284
Blain Change Framework 51–284
Buckminster Fuller 63–284
Buddha 184–284

C

Career and Life Game Change System 36–284
Carlos Casteneda 168–284
Charles Darwin 44–284
Charles Dickens 58–284
Chernobyl 126–284
Children's Society' 98–284
Chile 161–284
Clare Francis 114–284
Clinton Foundation 197–284
Cluedo 177–284
Cowspiracy 90–284
CRM 40–284

D

Dalai Lama 181–284
Dark Web 62–284
David Eagleman 146–284
David Schwartz 205–284
Davos 68–284
Despicable Me 198–284
Dinosaurs 87–284
DNA 72–284
Donald Trump 68–284
Douglas Tompkins 161–284
Downton Abbey 204–284
Dr Wayne Dyer 158–284
Duke University 89–284

E

Easter Eggs 160–284
Ebola 69–284, 96–284
Edgar Mitchell 144–284
Edmund Burke 69–284
Ellen Macarthur 169–284
Elon Musk 48–284
Elvis 44–284
Enlightenment 125–284

Erling Gudmundsson 229–284
ERP 40–284

F

Facebook 59–284
Fertilisers 163–284
Fitbit 221–284
Foxconn Factory 21
FTSE 100 52–284
FTSE 250 52–284

G

Galileo 50–284
Gary Dutton 42–284, 176–284
Genes 73–284
Golden Gate Bridge 268–284
Google 59–284
Greece 81–284

H

Harrison Ford 225–284
Hay on Wye 115–284
he Matrix 136–284
HMS Coventry 112–284
HMS Fearless 111–284
Hobie Skateboard Team 116–284
Homo Sapiens 60–284, 144–284

I

IBM 63–284
Indonesia 255–284
Internet of Things 63–284
Investment Bankers 52–284
IPO 41–284
Ireland 113–284
Isaac Newton 44–284
ISIS 62–284
Italian parliament 90–284

J

Jack Nicholson 24–284
James Bond 257–284
Japan 126–284
Jean Liedloff 75–284
Jeepney 199–284
Jennifer Aniston 225–284
Jenny 74–284
Jim Carrey 178–284, 225–284
JK Rowling 44–284
John Peck 248–284
Jonathan Baillie 89–284
Jon Bon Jovi 225–284
Jules Verne 229–284

K

Kanye West 225–284
Keanu Reeves 136–284
Kobe 126–284

L

La Gomera 248–284
Laurence Fishburne 136–284
Leon Festinger 102–284
Life Expectancy 79–284
Louis Pasteur 50–284

M

Mad Cow dDsease 126–284
Madonna 44–284
Magna Carter 139–284
Mahatma Gandhi 128–284
Make a Wish Foundation 23–284
Making the most of your life 20–284
Mark Urban 88–284
Mark Zuckerberg 180–284
Martin Luther King 220–284
McKinsey & Co 81–284
Michael Fassbender 225–284
Michael Jackson 22–284
Michael Johnson 43–284
Michael Jordan 44–284

Michael S Forbes 160–284
Michael Wilson 52–284, 263–284
Microsoft 62–284
Mike Weed 116–284
Milford Haven 115–284
Mobil Oil Corporation 117–284
Monopoly 177–284
Montessori 74–284
Morgan Freeman 24–284

N

Napoleon 139–284
Napoleon Hill 167–284
NASA 214–284
National Geographic 85–284
National Union of Students 98–284
Nelson Mandela 49–284
NHS 97–284
Nimrod 113–284
Nobel Peace Prize 49–284
North Atlantic Ocean 111–284
North Face 161–284
Nuclear Bomb 61–284

O

Oliver Sacks 211–284
Olympic 100–284
Olympic Champion 104–284
Oprah Winfrey 225–284
Out of the Shadows 97–284
Oxford University 72–284

P

Patagonia 161–284
Patanjali 168–284
Paul Ehrlich 88–284
Paul Lockyer 276–284
Philippines 112–284
Phishing 64–284
Ponzi 52–284
Population Reference Bureau
60–284
Premier League 100–284
President of the United States of
    America 140–284
Prince 22–284
Prince Harry 22–284
Princess Diana 192–284
Project Loon 62–284

Q

Quality of life 236–284
Queen of Great Britain 140–284

R

RAF 113–284
RAF Brawdy 113–284
Ray Anderson 85–284
Remote Tribes 158–284
Renault 4 111–284
Republic of South Africa 49–284
Rex Barker 227–284
Richard Branson 48–284
Richard Gere 228–284
Robin Williams 22–284
Roger Bannister 49–284
Royal Navy 111–284
Rudyard Kipling 44–284

S

Sandra Bullock 225–284
San Francisco 268–284
SAP 40–284
Sarah Johnson 22–284
Self Actualisation 207–284
Sharks 20
Shimon Peres 198–284
Simon Sinek 205–284
Sir Dave Brailsford 101–284
Sir Mick Jagger 57–284
Sir Phillip Green 70–284
Socrates 44–284

South Atlantic 201–284
South East Asia 112–284
South Wales 113–284
Stanford University 88–284
Stephen Covey 250–284
Steve Jobs 44–284
Steven Spielberg 44–284
St Helena 201–284
St James's Place 263–284
Strengths Finder 79–284
Stuart Pimm 89–284
Suicide 21–284
Susyono 255–284
Sylvia Earle 85–284

T

TED Talk 85–284
Telegraph Newspaper 81–284
Thailand 112–284
Thea Tagulao 276–284
The Bucket List 24–284
The Continuum Concept 75–284
The French Revolution 139–284
The Life Show 43–284
Time Magazine 85–284
Time Out of Mind 228–284
Trueman Show 178–284

U

Ukraine 126–284
UN 21–284
Universal Forces 166–284
University of Connecticut 88–284
University of Hertfordshire 162–284
UN Refugee Agency 21–284
USA TODAY 99–284

V

Vazhakodan Govindan 163–284
VE Day in Europe 139–284
Vincent Van Goch 44–284

W

Walt Disney 44–284
Warren Buffet 71–284
Wayne Dyer 158–284
Will Lankston 276–284
Witney Houston 22–284
World Bank 96–284
World Conservation Society 90–284
World Head Quarters 142–284
World Health Organisation 65–284
World Wildlife Fund 87–284
Wright Brothers 58–284

X

X Factor, 231–284

Y

YouGov 98–284
YouTubers 76–284
Yvon Chouinard 161–284

Z

Zika virus 96–284
Zoological Society of London'
    89–284

FINAL THOUGHTS

If You Don't Make A Shift And Change Now, When Will You?

Discover The Truth, Make The Connections And Change the Game.

Change The Way You Live Your Life And Manage Your Career Forever.

Orientate Your Life And Career Goals Towards: Happiness, Fulfilment And Making A Difference.

Embrace The New Enlightenment To Help You: Wisdom, Love and Imagination.

Find Your Own Path and Make The Most Of Your Life

When You Do These Things You Can Feel Good And Change The World

Get Help To Do It At:
www.FeelGoodChangeTheWorld.com
Join the Feel Good Change The World Movement

NOTES